Talks By Swami Paramatmananda

VOLUME 1

Mata Amritanandamayi Center
San Ramon, CA

Talks By Swami Paramatmananda
Volume 1

ISBN 1-879410-79-6

Published by
Mata Amritanandamayi Center
P.O. Box 613
San Ramon, CA 94583

Preface

Since 1968, Swami Paramatmananda Puri has lived the life of a renunciate in India, moving there at the age of nineteen, to imbibe the spiritual essence of that great and ancient culture. It has been his good fortune to have kept the company of many saints and sages over the years, culminating in his meeting with his Guru, Mata Amritanandamayi, in 1979. As one of her senior disciples, he was eventually asked to return to the U.S. to serve as head of the first ashram in the West, the Mata Amritanandamayi Center, where he has remained in residence since 1990.

Many residents and visitors to the Center have shared that one of the high points in programs there have been Swami's talks, encompassing his experiences in India, his understanding of scriptural texts, and his life on the spiritual path. With wit and humor, he has synthesized East and West, and created a forum for spiritual learning for people from all walks of life.

Originally available only on tape, his talks have now been transcribed, with his speaking style preserved as much as possible, making these volumes a treasury of wisdom for years to come.

Publisher
M. A. Center
March 1, 2000

Contents

Stories of Saints - 1

LAST WEEK WE TALKED ABOUT LADY SAINTS, lady *mahatmas*, particularly about some lady saints who existed in Vedic times, in very ancient times, who were Upanishadic sages. This week, I thought we could talk about some more recent lady *mahatmas*. Recent means about a thousand years ago.

We shouldn't think that every *mahatma* has to be a *sannyasi*, that one cannot become a saint or a sage or a mystic or a *mahatma* unless one renounces the world and puts on *kashaya*, puts on the *gerrua* cloth, the orange cloth. There have been so many realized people that were married, and they had children, they had a family and they had a job. And still in all the free time that they could get, they would spend in *sadhana*, in spiritual practice.

"You can't take it with you"

I personally knew a man, he used to live in Hyderabad. He was a professor, a philosophy professor. He happened to have a job that was very conducive to spiritual life. You would see him always doing *japa*. Whenever he didn't have to talk or whenever he didn't have to engage himself in something, if he was just sitting, or he was in a bus on the way somewhere, or he was driving his car, you would see always one hand was going like this—he was always going "Ram, Ram, Ram, Ram.." He was always doing japa. Every free moment he was doing japa. And every saint or sage that came to Hyderabad, he used to go there to visit them, to have their *darshan*. If they would come to his house, he would invite them to the house. Some sannyasis and saints he kept in his house for two or three years. The rest of the family wasn't very happy about it, but he didn't really care, because he had realized that he had to save himself, that whatever he had in this world, he should convert it to grace. Or, one step down, to *punyam*. Punyam means merit. You know, nothing is—you could say everything is—either meritorious or the opposite; it takes us closer to God or it takes us further away from God or the Self. Or you could say, it brings us closer to happiness or it is sowing seeds for our suffering—future suffering. So that which sows seeds for suffering is called *papam*. It's loosely translated as sin, but I don't know if that would be a very good translation because that particular word has so many connotations that many people don't like. Punyam means that which makes for happiness.

So, such people realize that their material goods—they need a certain amount for their material life, but whatever is excess— should be converted so that they can take it with them when they go. You must have heard the expression, "You can't take it with you." Well, you can take it with you. But before you take it with you, you have to convert it. You can't convert it after you go there. It's just like you're crossing the mountain range and you're going to some other country, and in the other country they don't have an exchange, foreign exchange system. So here itself you have to convert it to the currency that's valid there. And then when you go there everything'll be all right, you'll have plenty of money. It's just like that. Our actions, our wealth, our health, our everything, we can convert it now to punyam, or to grace, but we can't do it afterwards. Afterwards, when we're on the other side, when we've joined the majority, we're not going to be given the choice: "Well, you've got twenty-five or fifty thousand dollars in the bank—you had; you don't have it anymore—, would you like us to convert it and you can go to a higher plane of existence?" Nobody's going to ask you that. So whatever has to be converted, we have to convert it now itself.

So, some great householders—in fact most of the rishis, the sages of ancient days, were householders—but even present day, and all through history there have been—some great householders, they did that: they realized life is fleeting, any moment may be the end of it, and they got the most out of life. Not in the sense that most people think of getting the most out of life. But they prepared for the life after this life.

Story of Karekalamma and the mangoes

There was a lady like this; her name was Punyadavati. She has another name also; her name is Karekalamma. And she's one of the famous Shaiva saints, one of the—you know, in Tamil Nadu there's a tradition, the Nayanmars tradition, that is, great devotees of Lord Sankara Siva. And in the Siva temples you'll see—there are sixty-three of them, they're all *mahatmas* and you'll see there are images of all of them, not just Lord Siva in the temple, but on one side you'll see all these *mahatmas*. They wrote many songs and they were all mystics. So this Punyadavati was one of them, and she has a very nice story. It just shows you how appearances are deceiving.

She was the daughter of a very wealthy merchant in this place called Karekal. I believe it was some place near Pondicherry; it was ruled by the French. She grew up and was a very beautiful girl. Another merchant in another town wanted to get his son married to Punyadavati. So it was arranged, it was agreed upon, and the marriage was performed. And they were very happy together. I believe her husband's name was Paramadatta. And they were going along and leading an ordinary married life and everything seemed to be quite normal. Her husband also was a merchant. In fact, the father-in-law gave the son-in-law a lot of money and established him in business, and he was living in the same town, Karekal.

One day when the husband was sitting in his shop, some other businessmen came and they discussed some business deal, then these businessmen gave him two big juicy mangoes. So, he gave the mangoes to the servant in the shop and told him to take it home to give it to his wife and that he would have it for lunch when he came. So the servant took it and gave it to Punyadavati. She was busy with her cooking; she had just finished cooking the rice, but she hadn't cooked anything else.

Just then, one *sadhu* came, a Siva devotee. And he was standing by the door, "Bhiksham dehi ca Parvati, O Parvati Devi, O Divine Mother, please give me *bhiksha*, please give me something to eat." He was begging. So she came out. She's a devotee of Siva, no? She loves Siva. From her childhood she does Siva *puja* just like we were doing last night. So she came running out. She said, "Oh Swamiji please, come in, come in, come in. Please have a seat." She put rice there. There was nothing else. Maybe some pickles, I don't know. But there was nothing else cooked. If we had our cook Kamala there, there would have been plenty. (laughter) Kamala was not around at that time, and Punyadavati, she had only finished the rice. She remembered the mangoes were there. So she said, "I'll give him one mango as a side dish, and maybe some yogurt and he can mix the whole thing, it'll be delicious." So she took one of the mangoes and gave it to the sadhu. He ate all the rice and the mango and was very happy, he blessed her and went away.

After some time, around noontime, the husband came there, he had his bath and sat down for lunch. She served him rice and all the items that she had made. Then he said, "What about that mango? I sent some mangoes, didn't I?" She said, "Yes," and she came and brought the remaining mango and put it on his leaf*. He ate it and said, "Oh, this is very delicious. Bring the other one." She was in a fix. She didn't say anything. She could have said something at that time. She could've said, "I gave it to a sadhu." But somehow she was a little hesitant. She wanted to please her husband. So she went into the storeroom and started crying. "O Siva, O Siva—what am I to do? He's asking for the mango, we don't have the mango. I could've told him but I didn't tell him—now what am I to say?" She raised her hands and cried, "O God, please save me!" And then—suddenly a mango manifested in her hands. She was not so much wonderstruck—probably she was a little wonderstruck also—but she was very grateful. She took the mango, she went out and gave it to her husband. He ate it and said, "Oh, this is ten times as sweet as that first mango. Where did you get this? Is this the same mango that I sent? How could I have given two mangoes that were so completely different? I can't believe it."

Then she thought she'd better tell the truth. So she said, "The sadhu came—then I gave the first mango. When you asked for the second mango now, I just prayed to Lord Siva, He gave me the second mango." And he said, "Uh huh, sure. If He gave you the second mango, can you get another one

---

* People in rural India used to eat on banana leaves.

also, a third mango?" She said, "I don't know. I'll pray to God." She just moved aside and turned around in the corner and she was crying, "O Siva! Please save me from this situation!" Then another mango appeared in her hands. So she turned around and there was the mango. She offered it to her husband. He took it in his hand and it disappeared as soon as he touched it. Then he was not only shocked, he was afraid, because he realized that his wife was not an ordinary lady. He said, "Are you a goddess?" and then she didn't say anything. She didn't know what to say. So he made a decision then and there that his wife was a goddess, his wife wasn't an ordinary lady, and he was afraid to live with her as a wife. He was a merchant, he used to go here and there across the seas in the ships—as soon as he left, on the next ship, he decided that he wouldn't come back to Karekal. He went traveling around, he got a lot of money, and when he came back to India, he settled down in Madurai, which is quite a distance away from Karekal. And he married again, got a daughter, and he called the daughter by the same name as his first wife, Punyadavati.

In the meantime, Punyadavati was waiting for her husband to come home; he never came home. And after some years, it must have been five or six years, some relatives who had been to Madurai had seen him there, and they told Punyadavati, "We saw your husband there, in Madurai." So they decided they were going to send her there, and they hired a palanquin and she was sent with some other relatives to Madurai. They went and told him also, and when she arrived, he came running out with his second wife and his daughter, and as soon as she got out of the palanquin, what does he do? He goes up and full length stretches out and prostrates at her feet. She didn't like that very much. Because, before that, she was bowing down to his feet. And so she got very upset, she moved away, she said, "What is this?" Then he told the whole thing to the relatives: "This lady is not an ordinary lady, she's a goddess, and by her grace I got remarried and I had a child, and I worship her in my house as the goddess Punyadavati..." and this thing and that thing. She got so upset that she prayed intensely to Lord Siva: "Lord Siva, I was preserving my beauty for my husband and now he doesn't want me anymore. So let only You be my all in all. Take away my beauty."

Immediately she became all shriveled up and skinny, almost like a ghost. They say she became ghost-like. She became very strange-looking, like a ghoul almost and everybody kind of ran away from her. She was very happy, because this was the beginning of her complete renunciation. It happened. It was God's will. It wasn't her will. Then she walked all the way to Kailas, Mount Kailas in the Himalayas. It took her a very long time. She got the darshan of Siva there; she had a mystic vision of Siva. And then He asked her, "What would you like? I'll give you a boon."

She said—I'll tell you what she said; it's very nice. She asked for four things. One thing was, "I want constant *bhakti*. I want complete, permanent, continuous devotion to You. Because I think of so many things, my mind wanders around from one thing to another thing—I want that it should flow only towards You, just like the Ganga river flows towards the ocean, like that my mind should flow towards You, without a break." He said, "That's fine; you'll get it. What else do you want?" Then she said, "I don't want to be reborn anymore. Because there's nothing in this world that I want. I only want to be at Your Feet. And if I have to be reborn, if I still have some *prarabdha karma*, if some karma is still there, then let me always be conscious that You exist; let me not fall asleep in Your *maya* so that I don't know that You exist anymore and think that only this world is real, only this world is valuable. Let me have God-consciousness even though I am reborn." And then she finally prayed that she should be able to see the cosmic dance of Siva at all times. Now this could mean two different things. You might have seen the image of Siva as Nataraja; he's the king of the dance. And I believe we were talking about this last night—maybe we didn't get that far.

One form of Siva is dancing—He's got fire all around Him, and He's dancing, and this represents the dance of the universe. You know, every single thing in the universe is moving. There is nothing that's still; every atom is in motion. If it's motionless, it's not the universe anymore; then it's the absolute Brahman. So Shakti, or Nature, Mother Nature, is all a constant dance. It dances into existence, dances out of existence also. When the vibrations stop, that's the end of creation. Then it's what we call *pralaya*, a dissolution of the universe. And then again the dance starts.

This is one way of interpreting that she wanted to see the cosmic dance of God. In other words, she wanted to see the whole universe as the form of God. The other way is that she wanted to actually see that form, as Nataraja, as Lord Siva dancing in the *akasha*, in space. And so Siva said, "Yes, you'll have that vision; you'll have everything you asked for." And He asked her to go back to Tamil Nadu and to stay in a place which is about thirty or forty miles, I think to the west, of Madras. There's a temple there, a Siva temple, and she spent the rest of her life there in meditation and ecstasy. This was Karekalamma, one famous lady saint. She wrote about a hundred and twenty or a hundred and thirty songs which describe all her experiences and her mystic union with and vision of God. This is part of the Saiva literature, part of the literature of Nayanmars.

(Question in background)

This is somebody that lived about a thousand years ago. We know Mother; she's alive today, and she's the most recent of the lady saints or sages. Of course, most of us look upon her as Parashakti Herself.

Story of the woman who fed baby Rama

But I also met another woman who seemed like an ordinary lady. She was in Hyderabad—I used to spend a lot of time in Hyderabad for the first ten, twelve years I was in India. And this woman, she was a widow lady, and what she used to do is spend all her time either doing puja, studying *Bhagavata*, the Scriptures, or doing japa. She used to do, I think, about a hundred thousand japas; she used to repeat the name of God a hundred thousand times a day. She would get up about three o'clock in the morning and she would start then, until nine or ten o'clock she would sit there, like a statue, doing japa. And you can imagine, she made great progress that way—she started getting divine visions. And I saw her in Tiruvannamalai—somehow we became very good friends. She was an old brahmin widow—she was very orthodox, but she somehow became very affectionate towards me. She looked upon me as her own son. She used to come and cook for me, and I don't know what it was, it was just a very nice relationship with her. I could speak her language, Telugu, at that time—now I completely forgot that language. And I used to speak in a very simple way and she'd speak in a very simple way, and she used to tell me about her experiences. Sometimes you talk to people, so-called spiritual people, and they start to talk about all their experiences and— they're kind of unbelievable. You feel as if either there's something wrong, or they're trying to impress you or something.

A lot of people talk like that. But if you talk to a genuine, innocent person, you don't feel like that at all. You can tell that they're like a child. Real spiritual people are like children.

This lady was just like a child, and after we knew each other for some time, she started telling me what happened to her. And she said that she was very upset because she was a devotee of Ramana Maharshi, and she liked to do *atma vichara*, self-enquiry. But every time she would close her eyes to try to hold onto the I-thought, to try to see the Atman, this little boy would come, little Rama, about a three-year-old little light grey-blue Rama. And he would come and he would jump onto her lap and he would start to pull her clothes, and say, "I want some *payasam* (sweet pudding)! I want *vadai* (fried tidbit). I want *dosa* (sort of light, fried pancake). I want something to eat!" And actually she could see it, she would feel her clothes being pulled like that, and hear him crying, and as soon as she would open her eyes, he would disappear. And as soon as she would close her eyes, again she would be seeing that and feeling him pulling and hearing him crying, and she was very upset. Very upset—if that happened to us, we wouldn't be upset at all. We'd be very happy—at least something is happening, no? (laughter) But that's the difference between us and her, because she wasn't going to settle for anything less than Self-realization—*atma jnana*. She didn't even want the vision of Rama or Krishna or anybody else. Anyhow she was getting it, this little Balarama, baby Rama. And so she would get up and she'd go near the kitchen—and usually she wouldn't have to cook at that hour. It's too early in the morning. She would have to cook because if she doesn't cook and get the food, the payasam, ready, Rama won't leave her alone. There are many instances of this, you know, there's other saints that had the same experi-

ence. One of Ramakrishna Paramahansa's lady disciples had
the same "problem", you could say. Not a problem at all.

And then she'd cook the *payasam* and cook the *vadai*—
she didn't want it herself; after all, she was just a simple spiritual sadhak. For him she had to cook all these fancy dishes,
he wouldn't settle for anything less. And then, with her eyes
closed she had to feed him, because she could only see him
when her eyes were closed. And she couldn't even get any
rest, because if she closed her eyes to rest, then he also came
over there, laid down next to her, started cuddling up against
her, wanting to play, to hear stories. She was very upset and
used to tell me about it. She said, "What's going to be my
fate? I wanted to realize the Self, and I have to be playing
with God all the time? He keeps me cooking—every morning at four o'clock in the morning I have to cook like this.
What am I to do?" And what was I to say to her? That's even
more difficult, because I had no idea—I wasn't seeing Rama,
Krishna or anybody else! So I said, "Surrender to God's will."
What else could I say?

Finally one day she came and said, "You know, last night
a beautiful thing happened to me. I was meditating, and Rama
again came, and I was a little—I don't know, I was getting
frustrated, I didn't know what to do anymore. So I started
praying to my Guru, and my Guru appeared there, and he
had a big cooking pot." A huge pot, it was like this; you must
have seen some of the cooking pots in India, where they
cook for feasts; to clean the pot you have to get inside and
stand in it, it's so big. So there was a big pot like that—,
"Then he had a big stick and he was stirring whatever it was,
I don't know what it was. And I was looking at that and I
was wondering, 'What a strange thing Guruji is doing; I wonder what he's doing.' Then he called me over there, I looked
in the pot, he said, 'This is Mysore pak'—you know what

Mysore pak is, it's a kind of sweet— 'It's Mysore pak, but it's not ready.'" Then she understood what he was talking about: that she wasn't ripe yet for Self-enquiry. The sweet, that's the sweet mind, the evolved mind, the spiritual mind. So he's stirring it but it's not ready, it's not completely cooked. If it wasn't cooking at all, she wouldn't have seen Rama, Krishna, or anybody else. But because it was boiling and cooking, she was getting that vision, but it wasn't completely cooked. And she told me that after this vision, the vision of Rama as a baby boy stopped, and then her mind became almost still, like a calm ocean, and she used to sit there for hours and hours immersed in herself, in the Atman.

This was just an ordinary lady, nobody knew about her experiences—probably I'm the only person that knew. I never told anybody. In fact, you're the first people I ever told that to. I'm so sure that she wasn't telling anybody, because she had no friends. She didn't care about friends; she cared only about spiritual practice.

There must be so many like that, so many saints.

The lady who cured the Swiss boy's ear

There was another lady. One day we were sitting there with Mother, in front of the ashram, and there was a boy there, a Swiss boy was living there for some years, and he used to do a lot of meditation, and his body got overheated from meditating so much. Because of the heat, he started getting an infection in his ear—something was wrong with his ear. He was also sitting out there, some distance away from Mother and us, and a beggar, a beggar-lady, came walking in. That's not unusual on the sea-coast where Mother lives. Sometimes beggars come across the river and they beg their food in the village.

This lady just came from the seaside right up into the ashram premises. She had these completely dirty clothes, almost falling apart,—they were all torn; they must have been years and years old, and she must've been maybe in her seventies and she was bent over and had a little tin can in her hand for begging. She went over to this boy, the Swiss boy, and he didn't know what was going to happen. She just bent over, as if she was going to say something and then in the ear that he was having the infection, she just blew in there—whoosh, whoosh, like that. Without waiting for anybody to give her anything, she just got up, smiled at him, and left the place, as if she had come just for that, only to do that. And Mother was watching the whole thing. Then She turned to us and said, "Did you see that?" We saw it but we didn't know what it was that we were looking at. Then she said, "You know who that is?" We said, "No." Mother said, "She's never come here before." "Then, Mother, how'd you know who she is?" Always we ask these stupid questions to Mother. This, "How do you know?" I don't know how many people ask Mother, "How do you know?" Then, immediately after, they realize what a fool they are to ask her how she knows. She knows because her knowledge is born of intuition, not born of experience or inference or intellect or anything like that. So anyhow we asked Mother, "Mother, how do you know?" Then she said, "That was an avadhuta; that was a lady *mahatma*. She wanders around like a beggar. It's the first time she's ever come here, and she knew that his ear was infected and that was the only reason she came here. She didn't come here to get any food from anybody. Didn't you see the way she just blew in his ear and went away?" She said there were many, many people like that. In fact, she said there's probably one in each village, that we don't know about them—a *mahatma*, who looks like a ordinary person, and isn't.

"She was more than a hundred and fifty years old"

So, appearances are very deceiving. Many of you might have heard of Mayamma, who was living in Tamil Nadu also until recently—I think she passed away last year or two years ago. Mother spent some time with her. We used to go and visit her once in two or three years. She was also like that, a lady *avadhuta*. She looked like a beggar. She used to walk around with a gunny bag, and with the gunny bag she would run into hotels and pull the people's food off their plates, put it into the gunny bag, and then she would run out of the hotel. In fact, we had no place to eat when we were visiting her so we went into a hotel, and there were about twenty of us, and Gayatri was sitting there and Gayatri just got up to go to the bathroom and Mayamma ran into the hotel, took everything off of Gayatri's plate, and went out.

What did she do with the food, you know? She didn't eat it herself. There were about twenty-five dogs that followed her around. She slept on the dogs, she laid down on the dogs, she played with the dogs, and she fed the dogs in this way. This was how she fed the dogs, by getting the food from the hotels. And no hotel owner would stop her, because she had such tremendous spiritual power—nobody knows how old she was—she must've been—Mother says she was more than a hundred and fifty years old. If she touched somebody who was sick, they would become all right. She swam out in the ocean; she didn't wear any clothes. She was stark naked—she was a *digambari avadhuta*. Some people put clothes on her, but she didn't like that. She just liked to be without clothes. And she wandered through the town like that; nobody would disturb her. And then, she collected all the garbage from the city, put it by the oceanside, lighted a fire, and just sat there and gazed at it for some hours. Nobody knew what she was doing. Mother said that she was a great *mahatma*. Now she's left the body.

So there are many women like that. I wanted to talk about one of the greatest. I didn't get around to it today either. I guess we're going to have to wait till next week or it's going to be too late even for the *bhajans*. But I already told you last week who we were going to talk about this week, and who actually we're going to talk about next week—that is Andal. She was one of the greatest. There've been great ones, and then there's greater ones still, you could say. All of them have experienced God, but Andal, her fate was very, very rare, but I'm not going to tell you why now. You can hear that next week.

Namah Sivaya.

Satsang at M.A. Center, 1994
Tape 1 - Side A

Stories of Saints - 2

LAST WEEK WE WERE TALKING ABOUT HOW APPEARANCES are sometimes deceiving, especially in the case of spiritual people. And we gave some examples of women saints who appeared to be quite ordinary people and turned out not to be so ordinary. Today I'd like to take up where we left off last week.

Story of Tulasidas who wanted Ram's *darshan*

Many of you might have heard of Tulasidas. He has written a great book, *Tulasi Ramayana*, or *Ramacharitamanasa*, which is a devotional version of the Ramayana written by Valmiki. Tulasidas was a great devotee of Lord Rama and he spent many years trying to get the vision of Rama, but in spite of all his efforts, he couldn't get the divine vision. So one day he was coming back from the Ganges River—every day he used to go to the Ganga and get some water, so that after he would go to the toilet he would have the water to clean himself. As he was walking back, he used to throw the remainder of the water at the foot of one tree. One day as he was passing the tree after throwing the water, he heard a voice say, "I'll give you a boon." He couldn't understand where was this voice coming from. He went near the tree and again the voice said, "I'll give you a boon. What boon do you want?" Then Tulasidas said, "Who is this that's talking?" The voice said, "I am a ghost who is possessing this tree, who lives in this tree, and I've been very thirsty, and I'm grateful to you because you've been giving me this water every day. And so whatever I can do for you, I'm willing. I'll give you a boon." Then Tulasidas said, "I would like the darshan of Rama." The ghost said, "I can't do that for you, but I know somebody who can. That is Hanuman." Then Tulasidas said, "I also know that, that by Hanuman's grace, I can see Rama. But where's Hanuman?" So the ghost said, "You know, every evening you're giving a discourse on the Ramayana, and the last person to go after the discourse is over is one leper, and he's in the back of the room; that's Hanuman. He's coming just to enjoy the story of Rama, and he comes disguised like that. So you go there and you appeal to him for Rama's darshan."

So Tulasidas was waiting that night after he gave his talk—everybody got up and left, and the last person to get up was this person at the back of the room, the leper. So he went over to him and he fell down at the leper's feet and held his feet and he was crying, "O Hanumanji, Hanumanji, please bless me with your grace!" The leper was just standing there, and finally Tulasidas got up and the leper said, "I am nobody; why are you doing this to me?" And Tulasidas said, "No, I know you are Hanumanji." He kept persisting, and then finally Hanumanji said, "Okay, what do you want?" Then he said, "I want Ram's darshan." Then the leper said, "All right, you go to Chitrakoot"— (that's the mountain where Rama and Sita used to live for many years, which is not too far from where Tulasidas was. Of course, he was in Benares; Chitrakoot is some distance, but not unwalkable). He said, "You go to Chitrakoot and worship Rama there, and you'll get Rama's darshan, by my grace."

And so Tulasidas went there, he followed the advice, and sure enough he got the darshan of Rama, in a very strange form. He got two darshans of Rama. The first darshan was, he was sitting there doing Ram puja and a pig came running and knocked over everything and went off. Wild pig. Then he was very upset: his puja was spoiled, everything was dirty and smelly...Hanuman came there. He said, "Well, did you see Ram?" He said, "I didn't see Ram. Where is Ram? I've been sitting here doing puja so many days; I still haven't seen Rama. You promised me!" He said, "That was Rama. He just walked—ran—through your puja." Then Tulasidas said, "If he looks like that, how am I to recognize him?" So Hanuman said, "Okay, one more time you'll get the darshan of Rama." So he was doing puja another day, and so many people came there to get the *prasad*. Two young boys came there, one was fair and one was dark. Tulasidas was giving the prasad to everybody and he put the *chandanam*, the sandalwood paste, on the forehead of these two boys, and just as he touched them he realized that that was Rama and Lakshmana, and he became unconscious from ecstasy. For about two or three days he just laid there in that bliss of having seen Rama.

So anybody may be a Hanuman. That's the point. Anybody may be anything; you cannot tell who is who, because *mahatmas* are God and they don't wear signboards that say, "I am such-and-such." We just have to have that consciousness or that faith that anybody may be a divine soul. Ultimately everybody is divine, but those who are conscious of it, such people may take any form.

Unniappam Swami who saw Parashakti in the womb of Damayanti Amma

In Mother's life, there are two people that I am reminded of that, before Mother was born, were this type of persons. There was somebody who was living in the coastal area; his name was Unniyappam Swami. He was a very strange character; nobody understood what he was, most people thought that he was a beggar. But he had one unusual quality about him which made him stand out as anything but a beggar. He had matted hair tied on his head, which is not unusual in itself—so many sadhus do. But this Unniyappam, when he was walking along the seacoast, and the little kids would come and play and make fun of him—you know how little kids are, he would just stick his hands in his hair, and would pull out a hot, ready, cooked *unniyappam*. Unniyappam is a kind of a sweet which they cook in Kerala—in fact, I think we had unniyappams here one night. We had them cooked in the conventional way. (laughter) But he used to cook them in his own way. Just he would pull out nice, steaming hot *unniyappams* and give to all the kids. This is how he got the name "Unniyappam Swami".

So, I have heard that this person, one day, was walking down the seacoast and he came into the village where Mother was born. This was just before Mother was born. At that time, Mother's mother, Damayanti Amma, was pregnant with our Mother. And they were living just near the roadside of the path, just near the path that goes through the village along the ocean. They were not living where the ashram is now—they used to live on the ocean side. Now that whole area is gone; it's been washed away by the sea. This was before that sea wall was there. Damayanti Amma was just standing in front of the house and Unniyappam Swami walked by. He came over to Damayanti Amma and he gave her some ashes—you know, sacred ash, vibhuti, bhasma. And he said, "Parashakti is in your womb and She'll be born as your daughter." And then he just walked away. Well, we know that Mother was born from her, and so many miraculous things happened even when Mother was a child. Now, of course, there are thousands, maybe even millions of people that have the experience and have the belief that that's who Mother really is: Parashakti. But if you had looked at Unniyappam Swami you wouldn't have at all imagined that he could know such a thing.

There is an ashram under the present ashram

Then there was another person, and the person who experienced this was Ammachi's father, "Acchan" we call him, Sugunanandacchan. He was playing around in the front yard—this was when he was a young man—and this was in the other property, that is, where the ashram is now, not on the ocean side. They had these two properties. He was playing with a friend of his, they were climbing a cashew tree and one *sannyasi* or a sadhu came, and he stood there on the property and started laughing and laughing and laughing—you might have read this in Mother's life story. He was laughing, and Acchan asked him, "Why are you laughing? Are you making fun of us?" Then he said, "No, I'm laughing because I feel so blissful here. This is a holy place, and under this earth, so many tombs are there of holy people—so many sannyasis have been buried under here. There must have been an ashram here long ago." And then he just left the place. And Mother said that it is so—that under the present ashram, Mother's previous ashram from her previous existence was there. This is one of the reasons we feel so much peace and bliss in the ashram. Of course, it's mainly because Mother has been living there Her whole life, and so many sadhaks are doing so much sadhana there, but another reason is that it has accumulated from even before, a long time before.

We need not think that only old people can be *mahatmas* or saints or *avadhutas*; young people also can be like that. For example, Mother. Since she was a teenager, she has been manifesting the *bhava darshans*, and even though not everybody understood it, most people did accept that Mother was a great soul. You might have read in the *Kathopanishad*—for me that's my favorite Upanishad—the story of Nachiketas. That's the classical story of a young person who was a great saint. For those of you who don't know the story of Nachiketas, I'd like to talk about it and also read a little bit from the Kathopanishad.

The story of Nachiketas and the Lord of Death

Nachiketas was perhaps a teenager at the time, and his father was performing a big *puja*. And you know, in India when you do a big puja, part of the puja is to give gifts away, usually to the priests, or to the brahmins. Now Nachiketas' father didn't have much money, so he got some cows to give away, some cows that were completely dried up—they had no milk, they had no calves. What's anybody going to do with a dried up old cow? And he gave all these old cows away to somebody as if it was a very great donation, a gift. Nachiketas was having strong faith in Vedas; he had studied the scriptures—he couldn't keep quiet. It wasn't out of any arrogance—he just felt that he should say something to his father because what was going on wasn't good. He knew that if you give something that's bad to somebody, you'll get a bad fruit; if you give a good thing, you'll get a good fruit.

So, to protect his father, he said, "Father, this isn't so good. Maybe you could give me away to them." The father didn't say anything. Then again he said, "Father, who are you going to give me to?" Father didn't say anything. Nachiketas said it three or four times. Finally his father got angry with him. He said, "I give you away to Death." He just got so angry. He said, "I give you to Yama, to Death." And Nachiketas said, "Okay." He left the place and went to the abode of Death, Yamaloka. He reached Yamaloka and Yama was not there—he was not in his house, in his palace. So Nachiketas sat there at the gate for three days and three nights, and after three days and three nights sitting there, finally Yama came, and he was shocked to see him—"Oh, this poor boy, he's been sitting here three days!" And he immediately invited him in and said, "Listen, I want to do something for you, because three days and three nights you've been suffering, sitting at the gate, no food, no water, no nothing—you're my guest. So I'll give you three boons."

What were the boons? Nachiketas said, "Okay, my first boon: I would like when I go back, that my father shouldn't be angry at me anymore." Yama said "Okay, so be it. What do you want for the second boon?" And he said, "I heard that in heaven there's no suffering, there's no sorrow, there's not even death like there is on earth. So I'd like to know how to get to heaven—what's the means to get to heaven." So then Yama told him, "There is a kind of puja that you have to do. If you do that puja then that'll take you to heaven after you leave the body." So he taught him that puja—it was actually a fire ceremony—and he said, "And in honor of you, I'm going to name this as the Nachiketas fire ceremony. What would you like for your third boon?" So that's where we're going to start reading, when Yama asked, "What do you like for your third boon?"

Nachiketas says,

> "When a person dies, there arises this doubt. He still exists. Some say he doesn't exist. I want you to teach me the truth. This is my third boon."

So he's saying, some people say when you die, that's the end of everything—that's what materialists say. And some people say, you still exist after death. So, you're the god of death, you're Yama, you must be knowing better than anybody else. I want to know what happens after death. Well, am I gonna exist or no?

Yama said,

> "This doubt haunted even the gods, for the secret of death is hard to know. Nachiketas, ask for some other boon, and release me from my promise. Don't ask me this, please."

Nachiketas said,

> "This doubt haunted even the gods of old—because it is hard to know, O Death, as you say; I can have no greater teacher than you, and there is no boon equal to this. So, I don't want anything else, I want to know what happens after death."

He's very clever—no, not clever. He's—well, you'll see what he is.

Yama said,

> "Ask for sons and grandsons who will live a hundred years; ask for herds of cattle, elephants, horses, gold, land. Ask

to live as long as you desire, or if you can think of any-
thing more desirable, ask for that, with wealth and long
life as well, Nachiketas. Be the ruler of a great kingdom,
and I'll give you the utmost capacity to enjoy the plea-
sures of life."

What's he doing? Bribing him, right? Well, let's not use
that word. Tempting him. (laughter) But, yes, you could say,
sort of, he's bribing him.
   Nachiketas said,

"These pleasures last, only till tomorrow, and they wear
out the vital power of life. How fleeting is all life on earth.
Therefore keep your horses and your chariots, your danc-
ing and your music for yourself. Never can mortals be
happy by wealth alone. How can we be desirous of wealth
when we see your face and know we cannot live while
you are here? This is the boon I choose and I ask from
you. Having approached an immortal like you, how can
I, subject to old age and death, ever try to rejoice in a
long life for the sake of the senses' fleeting pleasures?
Dispel this doubt of mine, O Death: Does a person live
after death, or does he not? Nachiketas wants no other
boon than the secret of this great mystery."

So, what is Nachiketas? He's a first class spiritual aspirant. Why? 'Cause he doesn't want anything else. He wants
to know what happens after death. In other words, does the
soul exist? Am I the soul or am I the body that's definitely
going to die? He can't be tempted by anything else.
   Yama said,

"The joy of the Self, the Atman, ever abides, but not
what seems pleasant to the senses. Both these, differing

*in their purpose, prompt man to action. All is well for
those who choose the joy of the Atman, but they miss the
goal of life who prefer the pleasant."*

He is saying that we've got this choice, all the time, in
front of us—to choose the pleasures of life, which is quite
natural; everybody wants that—or, to try to attain the bliss
of the Self, which is very hard, but which will last forever.
And the pleasures of the senses, they come and go—you eat
something tasty, it's pleasant, then it's gone. Then again you
have to eat something, you can't do it immediately, because
the senses have to recoup—you eat again, and then again it's
gone. So it's fleeting. It's just for a moment. Every sensual
thing is like that: it comes, it goes. We would like to be able
to enjoy non-stop, continuous, day and night. But the very
nature of the senses are that they're fleeting—they can give
only temporary pleasure, and then they get worn out, they
get tired, then again they recoup. So it's endless. It's like a
bottomless pit; we can never fill it up. But the sages say that
if one attains the bliss of the Self, the Atman, then that stays
permanent—that's the essence of bliss.

Yama is saying that there is always this choice between
the pleasant and the good. This is called *preyas* and *sreyas* in
Sanskrit.

*"Perennial joy or passing pleasure. This is the choice one
is to make, always. The wise recognize these two, but
not the ignorant. The first welcome what leads to abiding joy, though painful at the time; the latter run, goaded
by their senses, after what seems immediate pleasure."*

We always are presented with this choice. Not just once
in a while; every moment of our life we have this choice,

either to run after pleasure or to run after the good. And what's good is usually very painful at the beginning, but at the end it will yield great bliss. And what's pleasant is very easy to get, but at the end, we have to suffer.

> "Well have you renounced these passing pleasures, so dear to the senses, Nachiketas, and turned your back on the ways of the world, which makes mankind forget the goal of life. Far apart are wisdom and ignorance. The first leads to Self-realization; the second makes one more and more estranged from his Real Self. I regard you, Nachiketas, worthy of instruction, for passing pleasures tempt you not at all."

So you're a good *sadhak*—I'm gonna teach you. There's no sense in teaching the science of Self-realization to a person who is a complete sensualist—because they're not concerned about that at all. One should have at least one percent interest in something more than that, to even hear spiritual talk, or read the scriptures. He's got much more than one percent interest, of course.

> "It is but a few who hear about the Atma; fewer still dedicate their lives to Its realization. Wonderful is the one who speaks about It; rare are they who make It the supreme goal of their lives. This awakening you have known comes not through logic and scholarship, but from close association with a realized teacher. Wise are you, Nachiketas, because you seek the Self eternal. May we have more seekers like you."

So how do we gain that knowledge? Mainly through the association with a Self-realized soul.

"Know the Self as the Lord of the chariot."

Now he's instructing him. He praised him for being a fit sadhak; now what is that Self?

> *"Know the Self as the Lord of the chariot, the body as the chariot itself, the intellect as the charioteer, and the mind as the reins; the senses are the horses; selfish desires are the roads that they travel."*

So, we are the charioteer; the body is the chariot; our mind and intellect are the things that hold the reins, and what are the reins connected to? The senses. And where do the senses go? Where do the senses go? (*Answer offered: "To the chariot."*) They're already in the chariot—where do they go? If the road is the sense objects, that's where they go—they go out along the roads, the senses. So the roads are the sense objects. Just as the sense of sight sees the objects, the nose smells nice smells, the ears hear nice music—those are like roads. And each one of the senses is like a horse. Then the mind is holding the reins, and deciding which one should go which direction. That's the meaning.

> *"When one lacks discrimination and his mind is undisciplined, the senses run hither and thither like wild horses."*

When one doesn't have any sense of control or discrimination, the senses just go any direction they want. You might have experienced that. Sometimes you walk through the kitchen, there's something tasty to eat, it's sitting on the counter, you just go like that. You were on your way somewhere else; then your eyes went like that, your nose went like that, your tongue is going to go like that after a few moments. So what's it due to? The reins are loose; the discrimination is gone. We just follow the senses. We do it all the time. The ears, the eyes—everything is like that; the mind just gets pulled whichever way the senses are directed.

> "When one has discrimination and has made the mind one-pointed, then the mind becomes pure and can reach the state of immortality. Those who reach not that state wander from death to death. But those who have discrimination with a still mind and a pure heart reach the journey's end and never again fall into the jaws of death. With a discriminating intellect as charioteer, and a trained mind as reins, they attain the supreme goal of life: to be united with the Lord of Love."

So when we have the reins in our hands, when our senses act the way we want them to rather than us acting the way they want us to, then the mind becomes calm, because the only thing that really agitates the mind is the wandering senses. If the senses get under control, then the mind also becomes calm. In that calm mind then, the Lord of Love, the Paramatman, we will see reflected in ourself. And that's the state of immortality, when we realize God.

> "Get up! Wake up!"

Not you. (Laughter) He's talking to Nachiketas—not that Nachiketas is sleeping. He's saying,

> "Seek the guidance of an illumined teacher and realize the Self."

Now here's a famous saying—you might have heard, and this is where it comes from:

"Sharp like a razor's edge, the sages say, is the path, difficult to traverse."

Spiritual life—the spiritual path—is as sharp as a razor's edge. That's very sharp.

"The Supreme Self is beyond name and form, beyond the senses, inexhaustible, without beginning, without an end. The Self-existent Lord pierced the senses to turn outwards; thus we look to the world outside and we see not the Atman within us."

The Lord made our senses work like that—our mind goes outwards, it flows out through the senses, so we miss what's inside, which is the Atman, the treasure.

"A sage withdrew his senses from the world, the world of change, and seeking immortality he looked within and beheld the deathless Self, the Atman."

So a spiritual person, an aspirant, a sage or a saint, with the desire to escape death—not the death of the body but the feeling that one dies when the body dies—a person who was inspired with that desire, he looked within, stilled his senses and looked within for the Self, and then he got the vision of the Atman and attained immortality.

Nachiketas says, "After that, how to realize that state?" Yama says:

"The Atman is formless and can never be seen with these two eyes. But He reveals Himself in the heart made pure through meditation and sense restraint. Realizing Him, one is released forever from the cycle of birth and death.

When the five senses are stilled, when the mind is stilled, when the intellect is stilled, that is called the highest state by the wise. They say yoga is this complete stillness in which one enters the state of unity, never to become separate again. If one is not established in this state, the sense of unity will come and go. The unitive state cannot be attained through words or thoughts or through the eyes. How can it be attained except through one who is established in this state himself? There are two selves: the separate ego and the indivisible Atman. When one rises above "I" and "me" and "mine", the Atman is revealed as one's real Self. When all desires that surge in the heart are renounced, the mortal becomes immortal. When all the knots that strangle the heart are loosened, the mortal becomes immortal. This sums up the teaching of the Upanishads. The Lord of Love, not larger than a thumb, is ever enshrined in the hearts of all. Draw Him clear out of the physical sheath as one draws the stalk from the grass. Know yourself to be pure and immortal; know yourself to be pure and immortal."

Nachiketas learned from the King of Death the whole discipline of meditation, freeing himself from all sense of separateness. He won immortality in Brahman, the Supreme Being. So blessed is everyone who knows the Self."

So, what Yama teaches him here—it's very clear: still the mind through spiritual practice; then one can gain the vision of God or the vision of the Self, and that itself is the highest state. Then the individuality subsides into the ocean of bliss. That's the state of immortality.

Nachiketas is one example of a young person in ancient times that attained that realization, and I've been promising you that I would tell the story about Andal, and I've kind of been dragging it on since I don't know how many weeks. So today we're also going to talk about Andal, because she was also a very young saint, just like Mother, in many ways just like her.

Story of Andal and Bhagavan Sri Vishnu

There was a *mahatma*—this was about twelve hundred years ago in Tamil Nadu near Madurai—many of you might have heard of Madurai. There was a group of saints. They didn't all live at the same time, but they were called "Alwars"— that means "the people who are immersed in God-consciousness." And one of them was called "Periyalwar"—which means "the elder alwar" or "the big alwar"—because he had a peculiar relationship with God. His attitude was—his aspect of God, his *ishta devata* was Krishna. But he loved Krishna like a parent to a child. So he used to worship baby Krishna, Bala Krishna, and he got the vision of God like that. So people used to call him "Periyalwar" because he was like the parent of God.

And Periyalwar was a very well-known person in those days, for his saintliness; even the kings knew about him and respected him. And he had a very nice sadhana. What he used to do is, he grew some gardens of flowers—planted flower gardens and tulasi gardens—tulasi is the basil plant which Vishnu likes very much, Krishna likes—and he used to make a garland, a big garland every day out of all these flowers, and then go in the evening and offer that to Vishnu, Lord Vishnu, in the temple.

One day he was out in the garden, removing weeds and digging up everything under the tulasi plants, and he found, strangely enough, a little girl, a baby girl. It was just laying there under the tulasi plants. And Periyalwar thought, "What is this?" He looked around, there was nobody, there were no parents, there was no—nothing. He thought, "This must be a God-given gift for me." So he took the little girl and started raising her. He called her "Goda". "Goda" means "born of the earth". In other words, as if she just sort of sprang out of the earth there. He raised her to be like himself, a devotee of God. She used to see how he was worshipping God every day, immersed in God-consciousness. So she also picked up all the same ways of life from him.

Goda had a very beautiful attitude towards God that was not exactly like foster-father's. She felt that Bhagavan was her beloved. She wanted to get married to Bhagavan. She wanted to be the bride of God. You might have heard of bridal mysticism—well, it's sort of like that, where you look upon God as your beloved and you want to marry God, become one with God, unite with God forever. So, she was having that attitude. It was natural to her, that feeling towards Vishnu.

Periyalwar would make these beautiful garlands, then put them in a basket. After going for his bath in the evening, he'd take them to the temple and offer them to God. When he would go out for his bath, Goda would take the garland, put it on herself, stand in front of a full-length mirror, and just look and be thinking, "Am I beautiful enough for Bhagavan?" She was wondering whether Bhagavan was going to marry her or not, and she was just seeing if she looked nice. And then she'd take off the garland and put it back in the basket before her father came.

This was going on for many days, and one day Bhagavan decided He wanted everybody to know about Goda's *bhakti*, her devotion. So, when Periyalwar took the garland to the temple one evening, Bhagavan made the priest notice one long, black hair in the garland. The priest said, "What is this? This is hair! Somebody else was wearing this garland! What kind of nonsense is this? Can you offer this to God? You already gave it to somebody else!!" And Periyalwar was shocked. He took the garland and went home. He didn't say anything to Goda; he thought he's going to try to catch her in the act.

Next day he made another garland, kept it in the basket and went out as if going for a bath, but he came around the other side and he was standing near the window. Then he saw Goda; she was putting on the garland, standing in front of the mirror and turning herself this side and that side. It wasn't out of any, you know, it wasn't that she was admiring herself; she was just wondering whether Bhagavan would be happy with her as a wife. And then he came rushing in. He said, "What kind of a sacrilegious—this—what's this—horrible! Who taught you this?" She felt a little shy, she didn't say anything. That night also he couldn't go and offer the garland to Bhagavan. He fell asleep. He was very upset. That night he had a very vivid dream.

Bhagavan Vishnu appeared to him and said, "Periyalwar, don't offer me any garlands except the ones that Goda has worn, because the fragrance of her love—it adds so much to that garland that I don't like the others anymore. So you make sure that she wears the garland first; then only bring it to me." He was a little surprised—to say the least! He realized that this child was a divine child, the favorite of God. He changed her name after that to Andal, which means "one who's immersed in the qualities of God." One who's full of God, in other words.

Andal used to go with her friends every morning (especially in the winter time, around December-January) to take a bath in the tank, the temple tank, and then they would go to the Krishna temple and sing songs to Krishna, asking Him to wake up, asking him to marry them, and to bless the world with peace. And these songs she wrote are beautiful—a song of thirty verses called Tiruppavai—and even now, though this was twelve hundred years ago, even today those songs are sung during that month in all the Vishnu temples in South India. In fact, all Vaishnavas, in their houses, sing these songs, they're so beautiful.

This was going on for quite a while, and finally she was a full-grown girl. It was time to get her married. Periyalwar also was getting a little worried, because she seemed almost crazy for God. He thought, like a lot of people think, "Well, if we get her married, she'll come back down to earth." So he started looking around for a suitable bridegroom and when Andal heard about it, she was quite upset.

You might have read in Mother's life story, how many times they tried to get her married. It was impossible to get her married. She put obstacles in the way every time. You know, it was very interesting, some of the things that she did. When they brought one boy to the house to introduce him to her, she stood in the kitchen window with a pestle, shaking it as if she was going to beat him to a pulp—this was the prospective bridegroom, and he disappeared like a bullet in the opposite direction. She did many things to discourage her parents from getting her married, until they finally gave up. They went to an astrologer who told them that they were very lucky that they didn't succeed in getting this girl married, because whoever the husband would have been, probably he would have died very soon afterwards. She was not intended ever to be married by anybody; she's a divine, yogic personality.

This person never met her; just from the horoscope he was able to tell that.

In the same way, Andal didn't want to get married. Periyalwar was a *mahatma*, not an ordinary person; he was not going to force her. He knew that she was a saint, so he said,

"Okay, what do you want? What are you going to do with your life?"

She said, "I want to marry only Bhagavan."

"Which Bhagavan do you want to marry?"

"Vishnu."

"Which Vishnu? There are so many Vishnus."

"What do you mean, there are so many Vishnus?"

"Well, there are so many Vishnu temples."

And he started telling about the different Vishnus—there's this Vishnu, and there's that Vishnu, and finally when he started talking about Ranganathan in Srirangam—there's a beautiful Vishnu temple in Srirangam—then she blushed. He didn't have to ask her any more. He understood that that's the Vishnu she wanted to marry. That's the Vishnu that she used to see in her dreams and meditations.

So he thought, "All right, how am I going to get this girl married to a stone? Impossible. Although Vishnu is not a stone, Lord Sri Ranganatha is definitely in the form of a stone. How am I going to get my flesh daughter married to a stone God?" He was in a fix. That night, he also had a dream. Ranganatha said, "Don't worry about it, I'll arrange everything." So, Periyalwar called all his relatives, they got Andal into a palanquin, and they started taking her to the temple in Sri Rangam. In the meantime, Sri Ranganatha appeared to the priests in Sri Rangam and said, "My beloved is coming, my bride is coming. Get ready for the marriage ceremony." And so when everybody met near the temple, the priests welcomed her with all honors as if she was the beloved of God. Still, no one had any idea what's going to happen, how this marriage was going to take place. Okay, at the most we make Andal go into the temple, we do some rituals and it will be over and she'll go back home with her father, she'll be happy for the rest of her life, she married God. That's what they were thinking, naturally. But that's not what happened.

They went into the temple, and when Andal saw Sri Rangnatha—she had never seen that image of God—she just was in tears and so much effulgence started to radiate from her. As if in a trance, she walked up to the image in the temple and stood next to it and started to glow more and more and more until she just vanished into light.

Everybody who was standing there was in shock. Especially Periyalwar who had lost his daughter. But everything became clear to him then, that she was the Divine Mother Herself.

This has happened to one other lady saint. I'm not going to tell you the whole story, but it is a well known story, about Mirabai. Mirabai also was mad for Krishna, and this is exactly the same way that she ended her life. She went into a Krishna temple in Dwaraka, she went up to the image and she merged in light. There's no samadhi, there's no tomb of Mirabai. Both of these lady *mahatmas*, they disappeared like that. There's a nice poem written by a Bengali *bhakta*, a Bengali devotee, in honor of Andal. After he read Andal's story, he wrote this little poem. And I'll read that to you.

Like some blessed fountain from the very core of your rich heart, O Saint, did you outpour you crystal holy love and ecstasy to God,
O bird with wings outspread in glee, adoration's summit did you overpeer and earth and sky were glad and evermore drink deep your song's ambrosial melody.

Your love was not of earth, no woman's soul for mortal
love craved with such a yearning.
So you did wed the great God himself,
O goal beyond our ken, beyond our dim discerning,
and soul to soul, like sunbeam into the sun, did you van-
ish away, O mystic One.

Namah Shivaya.

Faith in Mother

FIRST OF ALL I'D LIKE TO SAY TO EVERYBODY I'm very happy to see you and I'm very happy to be back. I spent one month in India. And, as I think most of you know, I went there because I hadn't been well in a very long time. Mother gave me one hug and that was more or less the beginning of the end of that problem. That leads me to what we're going to talk about tonight and that's "Faith in Mother."

Perfect faith is Self-realization

Mother says—and we know it, we're all spiritual minded—that the goal of human life is God-realization; that the thirst that we have for happiness, which never subsides whatever we may do, can be satisfied only in the bliss of God-realization. Because the thirst is infinite, only something that's infinite can satisfy it. So nothing we do that is finite, that gives a finite bliss, can yield the satisfaction we're seeking. And we can never turn off that thirst. We can never say, "Oh, I've had enough of this! I'm just going to be happy." You can't just be happy unless you merge into God, or unless you realize your real Self.

Mother says that for that to be possible, we need perfect faith. In fact, perfect faith is Self-realization or God-realization. That's a rather cryptic statement. What does She mean by that? At present, for us the world and the body are real. They're the only reality that exists. And God or the *Atman*, the Self, doesn't exist at all. It seems to be just an abstraction. You know, people use the word God in many ways, and that's about the only reality of God there is—just as a word, not as an experience. That's called *maya*, when we feel like that, that God isn't real and the Atman doesn't exist and the body, the personality, the world is real, that means we're under the influence of *maya*, the cosmic illusion. Because of that, we don't feel the infinite happiness of God-realization. So what Mother says is, we have to cultivate just the opposite, that God alone exists, that only the *Atman* is real, that the body, the personality, the world are unreal and just dreams in the cosmic existence, in pure consciousness. And not only think like that, not only cultivate that, but we have to live by that, which is even more difficult. In fact, that's the main difficulty in spiritual life. Spiritual life doesn't mean to just do a hundred and eight times your *mantra* morning and evening, go to the temple, offer a puja, meditate, go to the holy places, visit Mother. No. That's not everything in spiritual life. Real spiritual life means to live by faith, to live by that faith that God alone exists and only the *Atman* is real. Everything else is a dream. That's real spirituality, that's real religion, that's *dharma*, that's *tapas*, that's everything in spiritual life.

The atheist who fell off a cliff

Many of you must have heard this story, but it's very to the point. It's a very funny story also, about the atheist who fell off a cliff. He was running and he fell off a cliff. As he was falling down, he caught hold of a branch that was sticking out of the side of the mountain. He was clinging to that and about one thousand feet below was this abyss that he was about to fall into. He'd be crushed, shattered to pieces. So, as he was holding on, he was getting weaker and weaker, and couldn't hold on anymore. He was trying his level best to find some way out of this predicament. Finally, an idea occurred to him: "God!" Until then he didn't care about God. He never thought about God. And he thought: "God!" So he shouted out,

"Oh, God!"

No answer. And he thought,

"What can I lose? Let me try one more time. Maybe He didn't hear me. Oh God! If You'll just save me, I'll believe in You for the rest of my life. I'll spread Your glory all over the world!"

No answer. Silence.

"Oh, God, don't You hear me? Really, if You save me, I'll believe in You."

Silence. And after a moment a tremendous thundering voice came out of the valley,

"All of you say like that when you're in trouble."

The man was thrilled. He said,

"No, no, God. I'm different! I'll do whatever You tell me. Just save me and I'll spread Your name all over the world!"

The voice said,

"All right, let go of that branch."

The man said,

"What? Do You think I'm crazy?!"

That was his faith; that much faith only! Even when he heard the voice of God, he still couldn't obey that. More faith in the material world.

This is the crux of the problem. Mother is saying, "Have faith in God. Have faith in a God-realized Guru. That will be perfect. Everything will be all right. That's the magic key to becoming perfect, to becoming happy." But when it comes to tackling the practical problems with faith in God, somehow our faith goes down the drain completely and we're back in the world. We're all right as long as we're singing bhajans or we're in Mother's lap. Then it all just evaporates if there's a little problem.

In the *Gita* there's great stress laid on faith in the sense that, as per your faith, that is exactly what you are. In the eyes of God, or a God-realized soul, you could say that what your level is determined by is your intensity or your degree of faith. So Krishna says in the *Gita*, "The faith of each one is in accordance with his nature. The man is made up of his faith. As a man's faith is, so is he."

So that's what you are. What you have faith in, how much faith you have, that's exactly your stage in evolution, so to say. And all of us have faith in something always, because, as we are going to read now in Mother's words, you can't exist without some kind of faith. You would just cease to be. Why?

Faith is necessary for God-realization

One person asks Mother:
"Isn't it blind faith to say that there is a God?"
In fact, Mother is saying, there is no such thing as blind faith, or all faith is blind faith. Why?

"Children, everyone lives by faith."
These are Mother's words.
"Having the faith that there's nothing harmful in front of us, we take each step. We do not place our foot down if we think a poisonous snake may be in front of us. We eat food from restaurants because we believe that there

is no danger in doing so. But there are people dying from food poisoning, aren't there? Life itself would become impossible, if we did not believe blindly.

"When we get into a bus, we blindly believe in the driver even though he is a complete stranger. He might even cause several accidents. How many bus and car accidents occur every day! Even then, what makes us travel in a bus or car again? Faith, is it not? What about traveling in an airplane? Usually not even one person will escape alive in a plane crash, yet we believe that the pilot will take us safely to our destination.

"Take the case of a business man. What makes him start a business? Isn't it faith that he will be able to make some profit out of it? What guarantee is there that all these things will happen as we expect? None at all. So why do we continue to do everything that we do? Faith!"

But, Mother differentiates between ordinary faith in worldly things and faith in God or in spirituality, or faith in God-realized people.

"Real faith however is different from the aforesaid ordinary faith. Faith should be born of meaningful principles. Only then can it be called faith. It was through such faith that our ancestors lived abiding in God. None of them believed blindly."

So what does She mean here? That they didn't believe in God; they experienced God.

"Those who have seen God directly become witnesses to His existence. Their testimony does not become invalid simply because we have not seen Him. Those who have seen Him prescribe the way for others to see Him. It is not right to reject their testimony without following their

*advice on a trial basis, is it? Is it not a kind of blind faith
to reject something without experimentation?"*

So to say that, just because the *rishis*, or just because some
mahatma says that they saw God and that we should try to
see God also, and this is the way to see God, to say that that's
a bunch of nonsense—why should I believe that? How do I
know that they saw God?—it's similar to saying that your
grandfather said that he saw his grandfather. How can I believe it? How do I know that my grandfather saw my great-
great-grandfather? You can't prove that, that he saw your
great-great-grandfather. But he must have seen him. You accept his authority. In the same way, we accept the authority
of respectable people or sages, that God does exist, that they
saw God, that this is the way to realize God. Faith in a Guru
or a God-realized person or Master, is very essential. That's
the starting point for God-realization.

> *"To go to an unknown place, one must put one's faith in
> a guide. When such is the case for reaching a physical
> destination, what could be the objection to placing one's
> faith in a realized Soul in order to reach the supremely
> subtle and mysterious Reality?"*

"One has to be a child..."

Faith is necessary for God-realization, but it doesn't stop
there. Faith is necessary for any good quality life. In fact,
that's the secret to developing a perfect life, through faith in
God or faith in Guru. Mother continues to explain why that's
so:

> *"Faith in God gives one the mental strength needed to*

confront the problems of life. Faith in the existence of God is a protective force. It makes one feel safe and protected from all the evil influences of the world. To have faith in the existence of a Supreme Power and to live accordingly is what's called religion. When we become religious, morality arises which in turn will help to keep us away from malevolent influences. We don't drink, we don't smoke, we stop wasting our energy through unnecessary gossip and talk. Morality, or purity of character, is a stepping stone to spirituality.

"So faith brings these different stepping stones of real spirituality about, not to mention the benefit of keeping the mind peaceful and strong in the midst of the problems of life. We will also develop qualities like love, compassion, patience, mental equipoise and other positive traits. These will help us to love and serve everyone equally. Religion is faith. When there is faith, there's harmony, unity and love. A non-believer always doubts. He does not believe in unity or in love. He likes to cut and divide. Everything is food for his intellect. He cannot be at peace. He's restless. He always questions, therefore, the foundation of his entire life is unstable and scattered due to his lack of faith in a higher principle."

You know, here we used to read the Bhagavatam, Ramayana, Mahabharata, all these ancient stories that were written by the sages thousands of years ago. And it's told by the rishis that we shouldn't read these things with our intellect. We need not try to understand what's intended or even the inner meaning of the stories. We should read them just like children read children's stories, because that will make us like a child. Now, as Mother has stressed again and again last year when she was here, and the year before that—every year she's been stressing it—we're too much in the head. That's why we're not happy, because our heart is all dried up. All our concentration, all our attention, all the importance is in the head in thinking, understanding, knowing. But the feeling is not there.

We do need a little bit of that, something in the head. There's nothing wrong with the intellect, we need it. But that's not where the main show should be happening, so to say. The main show is in the heart. That's where God resides. That's where the *Atman* shines—not in the intellect. Intellect is just the assistant. To be like a child, then you can get that faith and happiness. No? What did Christ say? "One has to be a child to enter the Kingdom of Heaven." So simple, and all the sages have said the same thing in different words.

At that moment God lives in you

"A person who's endowed with real faith will be steadfast. A person who has religion can find peace."

We have to remember that when Mother uses this word religion, she doesn't mean just having a religion, believing in some religion. She means that having faith in God—if a person has faith in spiritual principles or in the Divine Being, even if they don't have any official religion—means a person is leading a life of religion. And she says here also, "A person with faith believes in unity, love and peace—not in division and disharmony." Mother is not talking about religion in the narrow sense but in the broader sense.

"Due to the lack of faith in a Supreme Power, non-believers will not have anything to hold onto, and surren-

*der to fully when adverse circumstances arise. As far as
a believer is concerned, God is the Supreme God. God
is the Supreme Being. God is an experience. God lives
in us, so a desireless love, compassion, forbearance, renunciation and qualities like these become present in us."*

This is a very nice statement of Mother's. Of course, everything that Mother says is very nice, but this particularly is
very nice. What she's saying is that when you express these
qualities, like desireless love, that means when you show love
towards anybody without wanting anything in return from
them, or you show compassion, or you're patient, or you renounce something that's harmful to you for your own good,
what happens is at that moment, God lives in you. God is
already in you, but God starts to shine through you, God's
presence starts to abide in you. You start to get to experience
the benefit of that kind of life. And that's the experience of
everybody. If they do any of these things, for a moment or
even for a longer time, they feel a kind of refined happiness,
not the happiness of getting and enjoying and taking, but
the happiness of expansion, which is much subtler. That's
gained through developing these principles or these qualities of spirituality.

*"If a non-believer has any of these qualities in him, he
will get all the benefits of a believer. What I mean by a
believer is not someone who has faith in a God, or a
Goddess, but someone who gives value to higher principles for which he is willing to sacrifice everything. If
these qualities serve as the principles by which the non-
believer lives his life, he'll be equal to a believer. On the
other hand, if those qualities are only on the outside, and
they're shallow and not deep, a person will not have the*

benefits of a true believer. Often non-believers like to talk but they do not put their words into practice. They are shallow and talk only to put on an impressive show. They do not have anything to hold onto. They lack the faith in the supreme Governor of the universe to save them from the problems of life."

Story of Job

There's a beautiful story in the Old Testament. It's the story of Job. Many of us are familiar with the story of Job, but it's worth repeating.

Job was a very virtuous person. He was very rich, *very* rich! In fact, he was the richest man in the state that he was living. He had thousands of cattle, thousands of sheep, tens of thousands of camels, and he was having plenty of money and land. He had ten children also. He was so virtuous that everyday he would do *puja* ten times a day. Why was he doing puja ten times a day? Because he had his ten children. He was worried that they were doing something wrong. So to make up for their wrongs, he used to do puja on their behalf. He knew that he wasn't doing anything wrong.

One day there was a *satsang* going on in *Brahmaloka*, just like we have satsang here. In the higher worlds, there are satsangs there also. Yes! Really! That's what the scriptures say. And God was sitting there, and many of the small gods came, the *devatas*, and some *rakshasas* came there also, you know, the demonic beings, the *rakshasas*, the *pisachas*. And the chief amongst them in the Bible is called Satan. He's one of the big shots in the *rakshasas*, he is the biggest. He's the head of the Mafia, you could say, head of the *rakshasa* clan. I don't know what he's called in the Indian scriptures. In the Bible he's called Satan. He doesn't necessarily have pointed ears and a tail and all that. We don't know what he looks like. He's pretty horrible to see, though, we know that.

Satan also came and sat there because there in that divine plane, they all take part in what's going on in that world. You don't have to be a great devotee to be there. Everybody goes there when they die. Not necessarily in Brahmaloka, but in the subtle worlds. Satan went there and he was sitting in a satsang, in the audience, and God asked him,

"Satan, where were you today? Anything going on, special?"

Satan said, "I was down on the Earth. I was just traveling around to see if there was anything I could do."

Then God said to him, "Did you see my servant, Job? He's my best servant. He's the best man on the Earth. Did you see him there?"

Satan said, "I saw him. What's so great about him? You pay him very well. Why shouldn't he worship You? You gave him all these properties and camels and children. Everything is there. Why shouldn't he worship You? If You really want to prove his worth, take away all his wealth."

Then God said, "Ok, you go and do whatever mischief you like to him, but don't hurt him physically."

Satan went back down to Earth. What happened?

Next day, Job was sitting in his house. He got the news: the cattle herd was struck by lightning, they were all destroyed; the sheep were stolen away by the neighboring tribes; the camels died of poisoned water. Not only that; that was bad enough, but the children were all in one of the brother's houses when a tornado came, knocked over the house, and everybody was killed.

What did Job say? What would we have said, if that had happened to us?

He said, "I was born naked, and when I die I'll go out

naked also. I came with nothing; I'll go with nothing. So what is there for me to say? He gave, God gave me everything. God took away everything that He gave. So let His will be done." This was Job's attitude. This is why God considered him His greatest devotee.

Next day satsang was going on in Brahmaloka and of course, Satan was there. He never misses a satsang! It's a chance to do some mischief for him. Then again God told him,

"Well, what happened? Did you see Job? What happened?"

Satan said, "Yeah, you're right. He's pretty good. But it's all right when 'things' are yours, but when it's 'yourself', that's another story. Now, if you let me make him sick, let me make his body really suffer, then, if he doesn't curse You, I'll agree that he's a great devotee."

God said, "Ok, you can go and do whatever you like. But don't kill him."

So Satan went down and he afflicted him with boils. His whole body from top to bottom was covered with boils. Well, you know how painful it is if you have only one little boil somewhere. He was covered with boils. They started to burst, they were oozing pus. Worms started coming there crawling in the wounds. That's what it says in the Bible. He was in such bad shape and it was going on for months and months. You know, for one week you have a boil—no big deal. But, if you're suffering like that for months and months and months... What happens? Your faith starts to get a little weak.

Some friends came to Job to comfort him. They heard that he had lost everything. He'd lost all his wealth, lost all his property, lost his children. He had nothing. Only his wife was there, and the house he was living in, and he was deathly sick, suffering so long. So they all came there and they started to comfort him And finally they said, "You must have done a lot of bad things to suffer like this."

Well, it's natural, when we see somebody suffering, we think like that: "They did a lot of bad karma, so they're suffering like this." But, you know, in the Bible, in those days they didn't believe in the theory of past births. You're born this birth and after you die, that's the end. You don't get born again. So Job was thinking,

"What did I do in this life? I didn't do anything wrong. Why are they accusing me like this?"

And they were giving so many arguments. "You know, if you just repent for all the bad things you did, if you just admit it before God, everything will be all right. It'll all disappear."

Then he thought, "I didn't do anything wrong. Why are they talking like this? Are you guys the only ones that know something? Am I so stupid? I'll teach you a few things about the ways of God and all that. You think you're so wise. You know it all!"

And then he started to complain to God and this is what he said. This is very nice because those of us who've suffered a lot, we also sort of do a similar act. It happens to come out like this, if our faith isn't real strong. So what does Job say?

"Oh God, am I some kind of monster that You torture me like this? You've taken away my family and my wealth and You've turned me into skin and bones because of my so-called evil deeds. I was living quietly until You broke me apart. You have taken me by the neck and dashed me to pieces. And then hung me up as Your target with Your archers surrounding me letting their arrows fly.

"Yet, I'm innocent! You don't even let me sleep peacefully, but give me nightmares! Must You test me every moment of the day? Did I hurt You, the All-powerful? And, if

You accuse me of doing wrong, what can I say? I can't even defend myself against Your accusations because You are not a man like me. And we could not discuss the matter fairly there being no possibility of having an umpire between us.

"Don't just torture me! Tell me why You are doing it. You have made me and You are destroying me. It is better that I die."

And to his friends he said, "What miserable comforters are all of you! What have I said that makes you speak so endlessly? Are you the only ones that know anything? Do you have a monopoly on wisdom? Don't I know anything? Stop accusing me of wicked things! I know what's right and I know what's wrong! And I'll teach you a few things."

So he didn't quite curse God, but he was about to fall over the cliff, so to say. He was on the verge of cursing God. These are all the objections that we raise also when things are really going bad. "Why are you treating me like this? You created me. And, at least if You'd tell me why I am suffering like this I wouldn't mind so much, but what's the use of suffering and not knowing why you're suffering. And what's the benefit of all this!"

This is what happens. These are the arguments that come up in our minds when our faith gets weak.

Satan almost won. And also what happened, Job's *ahamkara*, his ego, his arrogance, his pride, all the bad qualities that are inside everybody, they came up under the force of suffering—which is one of the reasons that suffering comes—so that all of that stuff comes out. That's what Mother says: whatever is inside has to come out. Then, when it comes out, if you know how to handle it properly, if you understand what this is and then you decide, "I'm not going to let this take hold of me, I'm not going to let it happen again," then you're rid of it. You become clear, so to say, like an ink bottle. You pour water into an ink bottle, and finally all the ink comes out, and then clear water is flowing. When all this rubbish comes out through the force of suffering, then it's like a clean bottle, so to say, and the presence of God can shine in there.

So all his stuff was coming out. And, when all of it had come out to the maximum, then God spoke to him. It was a whirlwind, like a tornado. And His voice came out of that. And He said, "Why are you using your ignorance to deny My wisdom? All these ignorant arguments you are giving to say that I don't know what I'm doing with you. What do you know? Now get ready to fight, for I'm going to demand some answers from you, and you must reply.

"All right, you arrogant fellow. You're telling everybody you know so much you're going to teach them! Now, you teach Me. I'm going to ask you some questions.

"Where were you when I laid the foundations of the Earth? Do you know how the Earth's dimensions were determined and who did the surveying? Do you know who is the engineer? Who decreed the boundaries for the oceans? Has the location of the gate of death been revealed to you? Who dug the valleys and who made the sun? Who laid down the path for lightning and the rain? Who gives intuition and instinct? Who provides for the young of animals?

"Do you still want to argue with Me? Do you, God's critic, have the answers?"

So what would we have said if we heard that voice? If we're smart, if we have learned our lessons, we'll say exactly what Job says,

"I'm nothing. How could I ever find the answers? I lay my hand upon my mouth in silence. I've already said too much."

Then God said—He didn't stop. He saw there was still some ego in him—so He said,

"Stand up like a man and fight! Let Me ask you some more questions. Are you going to discredit My justice and condemn Me without a battle?"

"I'm sorry, Lord, I know nothing. In my pain I uttered many unbecoming things. Have mercy on me, Your child."

God was pleased. Job became so humble. He became like a child. That's the purpose of difficulties. That's the purpose of suffering. It's just to make us humble like a child so that faith can blossom, so we can feel the bliss of Divine Presence. Then God blessed him. that all his land, all the animals should be come again. He had another ten children after that. He had a big family. And he lived for one hundred forty years. He even saw his great-great-grandchildren also—after he learned the lesson. And he died a peaceful death.

If we're having sufferings—and everybody has sufferings, there's nobody who doesn't suffer in some way or other at some time or other—we shouldn't curse God or curse our Guru, or curse Mother. We should remember that the purpose is to purify us, to make us humble so that we can get faith and enjoy the bliss of God-realization.

In the Gita, one of the last things that Krishna says is,

"The man who hears this teaching, full of faith and free from malice, even he, liberated, shall attain to the happy world of the dharmic Source."

With full faith, if we follow the path of faith, then we'll attain the divine world and we'll even merge into God.

Namah Shivaya!

Developing Will-Power

THIS IS NEW YEAR'S DAY, AND ONE NICE TRADITION in the West on New Year's Day is to make New Year's resolutions. We need not think that that's just a Western tradition. In fact, it's a spiritual tradition. It's not something unique to the Western world on New Year's Day. All of us every day are supposed to review what's good and what's bad in our mind; what's taking us forward and what's taking us backwards. Then when we go to sleep at night, make the resolve that tomorrow I'll be better. And that when we get up in the morning, to think, "Okay, today I'll conquer my weaknesses and cultivate good qualities."

But it's funny here, on New Year's eve, everybody just sort of throws away everything and then the next day they decide that they are going to become better from that day onwards. It's a funny aspect of human nature. Even though we decide that we're going to get rid of our negative tendencies, our *vasanas*, we find that our resolution doesn't last very long. That's usually the case with New Year's resolutions. Why don't they last very long? There are a number of reasons, and that's what we are going to talk about today.

Vasanas are like the bear

The main reason is that our will power is not very strong. Our mind is weak. Will power means to be able to put into practice our good intentions. But we're not usually able to do this. Why? Because our mind easily gets distracted. This is what spiritual practice is all about. We may want to get rid of a bad habit, but the bad habit doesn't want to leave us.

There's a story:

Two poor sadhus were swimming across the river. Something came floating down the river. One of the sadhus thought, "It's a blanket. Oh great! I can get a blanket. I didn't have a blanket until now." He caught hold of this thing and the thing started taking him down the river. Then the other sadhu said, "Come on! We have to cross the river. Let go of that thing!" Well, that thing which he thought was a blanket was actually a bear. So he shouted to his friend, "I want to let go of it, but it's not letting go of me."

So vasanas are just like this. We want to let go of them, we want them to go, but they're not letting go of us because many years we've been cultivating them, we've been developing them, we've been fondling them and kissing them, and so they don't want to go so easily.

There's a saint that gives a suggestion how to get rid of the vasanas. He says that when they come up, you have to mercilessly beat them. Of course, not with a stick or anything because they're immaterial, they're subtle, they're in the mind. A person who has a dog and he's always fondling the dog, kissing the dog, hugging the dog and doesn't realize that the dog is an irrational creature and may bite him one day. He has a friend and the friend comes to him and says,

"Don't you know you may get bit! You shouldn't fondle that dog like that."

Just like this person, he takes the advice and next time the dog comes he says,

"No! No! Sorry, you can't jump on me! You can't kiss me!"

The dog just jumps on him anyhow because he doesn't know. Our vasanas are like that. We may make a decision: "I'm not going to do this thing, or I'm not going to talk like that or I'm not going to look over there, or I'm not going to eat this thing."

We've made the decision, but the vasanas don't know anything about it. So then when the cake comes, or the person that we don't like comes, we eat the thing, or we say the thing impulsively, because we did it so many times, because vasanas don't know, they're just a habit. So what you have to do is give it a hit. If you don't want the dog to jump on you, you may have to hit it. It's not cruel. You have to teach it a lesson. And, if it still jumps on you, you have to hit it again. So, some bad habits—we have to be merciless about routing them out. They will come again and again until they get the idea, and then they'll stay away.

One reason why we can't get the strength of mind is, we're not so serious about it. Unless we're very serious about culturing our mind, it will be very difficult to conquer the mind. It's a full time job. You can't go one step forward and ten steps backwards and expect to get the mind to attain concentration and peace. And a mind that's cultured, a mind that's strong, is a mind that's peaceful and happy. So we have to have that requisite seriousness for that. That's why people take New Year's resolutions and they don't succeed, because they're not serious about it. It's just today they feel like that, but not tomorrow or the day afterwards.

For a spiritual person it has to be not just today and tomorrow and the day afterwards. Every minute until the last breath, we have to be trying to purify the mind. This is what it's all about. Purity of mind. Purity of mind means the power to control the mind and make it do what we want rather than having it do what it likes. And to be able to not think, to exist with a thought-free mind, just awareness, peaceful awareness without thoughts. We can think if we want to, but we don't have to helplessly think.

Feeling the burden of the ego

Unless we reach a certain state where we feel, "What a burden my mind is, all these bad habits that I have. How heavy they are! What a source of suffering they are to me," that requisite seriousness won't come. That's the stage. Just like an airplane is coming down the runway, it's about to take off, so, if we want to control our mind, we also have to reach that point where we feel that the ego is such a burden. Not the pure ego—the pure ego's okay. The pure ego will help us. But the negative ego, the ego full of negative qualities, until we feel, "Oooh, what a headache this is! Again I said like that! Again I did like this!" and we feel the suffering of our impulsive actions, it's very difficult to get serious.

Mother has something to say about that:

> "*If the goal is to realize the Supreme Being, you should become completely egoless. That requires self-effort. The sadhak himself must pray sincerely for the removal of his negative tendencies. He should work hard. This prayer is not to achieve anything, or to fulfill any desire. It is to go beyond all achievements. It's to transcend all desires. It is an intense longing of the sadhak to return to his original and real abode. He feels and becomes aware of the burden of his own ego and this feeling creates a strong urge to unburden its heaviness. It is this urge which ex-*

presses itself as prayer. Removal of the ego cannot be attained through the prayers of another limited soul. It takes self-effort and the guidance of a perfect Master."

Sometimes people say, "Please pray for me." Mother's saying that prayers done for others are effective for everything except this, getting rid of the ego. We can pray for others' health, and others' wealth, or others' well-being, but when it comes to removing the ego, each one has to do it himself. Nobody else except the Guru can do it.

"So the prayers of another limited soul will not help that. Working on the ego or emptying the mind becomes easier in the presence of a Divine Master. Even though Mother has said that somebody else's prayer cannot help remove another person's ego, a Realized Guru's mere thought, look or touch can bring about a tremendous transformation in the disciple. If he so wishes, a real Guru can even bestow Self-realization on the disciple or devotee. He can do anything he likes. His will is one with God's will. Praying for the fulfillment of petty desires is being stuck to your mind and all its attachments and aversions. Not only that; it is adding more to the existing vasanas."

We're talking about habits, vasanas, bad habits particularly. When we use prayer as a means to control our mind, or as a means to purify our mind, we should pray for the highest thing, not for lesser things, because lesser things just increase our desires, our vasanas. So it's amounting to praying to God to increase our bondage and our suffering when we pray for anything less than God-realization. If we make that choice, it's all right, nothing wrong with it. But for one whose goal is to realize the bliss of God, if one feels that that's the ultimate, then one has to pray only for that.

"New desires, new worlds are created. Along with that, you lengthen the chain of your anger, lust, greed, jealousy, delusion, and all other negative traits. Each desire brings with it those negative emotions. Unfulfilled desires result in anger. In contrast to that, when one prays for purification for the purpose of creating Self-realization, or awareness of the Self, the vasanas are destroyed. Such prayer will totally change your outlook toward life. The old person dies and a new one is born. However, praying for the fulfillment of petty desires does not involve any change in one's personality. The person who prays in this way remains the same. His attitude remains unchanged."

Many people say, "I've been praying to God for so many years and still I'm not making any spiritual progress. I go to the church every week, every Sunday. I do this and that and meditate." Why? Why don't they make any progress? One reason is this, that still their mind is occupied with, as Mother says, "petty desires," not the highest desire for God.

So this control of the mind, either through prayer or other means, is not just for us, not just for devotees, not just for spiritual people. It's for everybody. Because if you can't control your mind, there's no way to succeed. It will always be distracted by various things, and the goal that you set before you won't be possible to reach.

You have to apply the means

In the *Yoga Sutras*—many of you might have heard of it, it's the most authoritative text on meditation; it was written thousands of years ago by a great sage named Patanjali—the very first verse says, "yogascitta vritti nirodhah" which means,

"Yoga is control of the modifications of the mind." That's the real meaning of yoga. Today the meaning of yoga has just become doing yogic postures. But the real purpose of the postures and all the branches of yoga is to control the waves of the mind, to bring the mind to a standstill, to make the mind perfectly peaceful. In this yoga, in this system, you could say, of controlling the mind, there are steps. Many of you are aware of what those steps are, but today I thought we'd talk at least a little about them. We'll go into more detail some other day. That itself can be a series of talks about the *Yoga Sutras*.

Basically, if you want to attain an end, you have to apply the means. That's a scientific approach. And that applies just as stringently to attaining peace of mind. It can't be done haphazardly. It has to be done according to science. So the science of yoga and meditation, says that the first steps are what's called *yama* and *niyama*. Now, it's not the same Yama that comes and gets us when we leave the body, the god of death, Yama. It means restraint. The restraints are the yamas. The observances are the niyamas. It's like the do's and the don'ts of spiritual life. Most people meditate, they read spiritual books, they do a lot of things, and they neglect the yamas and the niyamas. It's like neglecting the foundation and then building a house on sand. I don't know how many people I've heard come to Mother and say, "Mother, I've been meditating thirty-five years, and I don't have any experience!" Why? Because the foundation was neglected. Just meditating is not enough. Just doing bhajans is not enough. The foundation, the yamas and the niyamas have to be attended to and if they're attended to, if these basic things are done properly, the next step automatically comes. Meditation will come automatically. No separate effort has to be made for that. That's not to say that we shouldn't meditate. We should meditate but, at the same time, we shouldn't neglect the basics, the foundations.

What are the *yamas*?

> *Ahimsa*: non-injury
> *Satya*: truthfulness
> *Asteya*: abstention from stealing
> *Brahmacharya*: continence
> *Aparigraha*: abstinence from avariciousness

Each one of these could take a whole day to explain, but, in brief:

Non-injury means not to harbor a thought of injury, even a thought, to any living thing, to anything in the world, anything in the universe, even in thought, much less in word, in speech, or in action. That's called non-injury. Just imagine, if we can perfect ourselves in anyone of these disciplines, how pure our mind will be; how much the vasanas will be removed!

Satya means truthfulness. Truthfulness doesn't mean just not telling lies. Truthfulness is the speech which will help us and help others go towards the truth. So if it's unpleasant, this is what the Scriptures say, if it's an unpleasant truth, it shouldn't be told. Just because it's truthful, you don't go and tell people their faults. That's a very common thing. Always we meet somebody who will tell us about ourselves, criticize us, or they criticize others. And that, even if it's true, is not to be done because the reaction which it causes takes a person away from the truth. So don't tell an unpleasant truth. It's better to keep silent than to create waves like that. Some people ask, "Shouldn't I tell the truth? Shouldn't I tell them that they're doing something wrong?" No, don't tell unless you are asked. If you're the person who's asked, if that person has confidence in you, then you can tell them because then it won't create a negative wave in them. It won't make them angry. Otherwise it's none of your business. Mind your own business!

And then, asteya, abstention from stealing: that means not even to think when you see a thing, "Oh, I'd like that!" when it belongs to somebody else, much less taking it, not even the thought, "Oh, that's nice." No. If it's nice and you want it, then go out and get one. Don't take somebody else's.

Then brahmacharya, that's continence. Continence means that even in thought one's mind is established in God, not in sexual things, physically, mentally and even the subtlest movement.

And aparigraha, abstinence from avariciousness. So what's necessary for me? That much only I want. I don't want any more than that because more than that entails so much of work and strain and unnecessary waste of life.

So we may feel, after doing these things a little, "I've done it enough. I've reached some stage, now I'm happy." It may not be good enough. The same Yoga Sutras tell you when you've had enough. That means, when you're perfect in these things, you'll know it. Non-injury, for example; when you're perfect in non-injury, then all beings that come near you, they cease to be hostile. It may be a tiger. You must have heard stories like this, no? Yogis that were walking through the forest or living in caves with snakes, cobras, tigers or lions, and other ferocious animals or even ferocious people. Because their mind was always established in non-injury, they never had a feeling of injuring another; then those beings also became harmless in front of them.

Last year we were telling the story about the cows here, you remember that? One day we were trying to get the cows into one place. There were some cows here. And usually you can just walk by the cows and they won't move. You can't go up and pet them, even some of them you could pet because they're all wild cows, but you could walk by them. I remember once I was sitting out in the field. I was talking to somebody there, and the cows were just two or three feet away. They were standing right there next to me. But this day we wanted to get the cows somewhere. And, you know, I came out of the house with a stick. The cows were about a hundred yards away from me. As soon as they saw me, they went running. They couldn't have seen that stick. I was just dragging it along behind me. They knew that I had some idea in my mind: "I'm going to chase them. If they don't cooperate, I may have to hit them." They intuitively knew that. Their power of intuition is much more than ours. Because they don't speak, their energy doesn't dissipate like ours. They depend on their intuition.

But this is just a practical thing. When I didn't feel that idea at all in me, the cow was right next to me. It wasn't going anywhere. I could have been talking and shouting in a loud voice to somebody and it wouldn't move. So they know. Every living being knows when "this person is a threat to me. I'm going to do something or I'm going to leave." Intuitively beings know that. So, if you're really established in harmlessness, non-hurting, then all living beings will become harmless before you.

Then truthfulness. When you have that kind of speech, that you don't tell a lie; that what is in your mind, and what happened and what comes out in speech are all one thing; and you don't speak unpleasant things even though they're truthful, then you get a power that whatever you say will come true. Just like Mother. She may say, "Don't worry. You'll become better, you'll become better." If she said that, you have to become better. Nobody knows when. She's not telling you when, but you'll become better. For sure it will happen because she's got the power of truth.

And then non-stealing. That's a very interesting one. It says in the scriptures that, "One who's established in non-stealing, to such a one, gems come." The word is *ratna*, gems. Strange, no? What is a *sannyasi*, a monk, going to do with gems? But the meaning of gems is not these precious stones. When a person is established in non-stealing, they have such a look of innocence, such a look of disinterestedness and detachment that other people are inspired with trust toward them. Then they feel inclined to give all the best things to such a person. Either just to share with them, or to entrust with them, as a trustee, because they know intuitively, this person is not going to steal this, he is not going to take it, he is so detached. Then all the best things come to such a person. This is the meaning of the gems, the ratnas, the best.

And then continence. When one is perfect in that, when one doesn't have even a sexual thought, what happens? One gets spiritual energy, spiritual power. Such a person, when they have that power of continence—it's called *virya*—then when they talk to you, those words pierce your heart. The same thing could be said by somebody else standing right next to that person, and it's just as dull as can be. Why? It's not because of the style or the words. It's because of the power behind it. It's not even the feeling of the speaker. It's the spiritual energy which they've developed through *brahmacharya*, continence. People won't even know why they feel that way. It's due to the spiritual energy of the person. That will sublimate us. When we hear that kind of talk, that's a real *satsang*. Then we'll forget everything, we'll live in a spiritual world. That's the spiritual energy of the speaker, if they have that.

And then non-covetousness: this is also very interesting. Patanjali says that when you have become perfect in non-covetousness, you get one *siddhi*. Siddhi means a mystic power. After all, these mystic powers, they are not mysterious; they're latent powers in everybody. They're just the powers of the mind, but because the mind is so scattered, we don't concentrate, so those powers don't manifest. They come only when we get concentration, when the mind becomes strong and doesn't think so much. Then the siddhis manifest. So, when you develop the quality of non-covetousness, when you don't want anything except the minimum for yourself, what happens is that you become detached from the world. You don't care about anything. And when you become detached from the world, the next thing is you become detached from your own body. Just the minimum is enough: a place to live, something to eat, a place to sleep, minimum. And when you become detached from the body then the real knowledge starts to shine. And the particular siddhi that Patanjali talks about is, the knowledge of the past and the knowledge of the future. This knowledge starts to dawn on the person who's established in non-covetousness. Because of their detachment from this world and from their own physical frame, the knowledge of the past and future comes. Why? Because they're not concerned even with the present anymore. They're detached.

These are the qualities of yamas. Then there's the niyamas:

Saucha—cleanliness. Cleanliness means both physical cleanliness and inner purity of mind.

Santosha—contentment. That's feeling I have enough. Why should I feel restless about getting this thing and that thing more? It's called *santosha*.

All these things are conducive to controlling the mind, making it peaceful.

Tapas—austerity. Nowadays tapas is used as a thing like suffering, "Oh, what a *tapas* that was!" But it doesn't mean suffering. On the other hand, it means the capacity to bear suffering. When it's cold, not to get upset, "Oh, it's so cold! It's so hot!" like that. Or, I have a headache, "Oh, what a terrible headache!" To be even-minded amongst all these opposites, the *dvandas*, the opposites, that's called tapas. To maintain, as they say in America, to maintain your cool under all circumstances, to keep an even mind, that's called tapas.

And then—*svadhyaya*, that's the study of the scriptures, the writings of the sages and *mantra japa*, both these things. Study of the scriptures doesn't mean reading all the spiritual books that any spiritual person has written, because if you go to any bookstore, you'll find hundreds, thousands. Nowadays everybody writes spiritual books! And everybody reads spiritual books. But that's not what svadhyaya is. Svadhyaya is reading the books written by *rishis*, books written by realized souls, not just anybody who knows something about something. The power of the word of a realized person, ancient or modern, is so strong. And then to repeat your mantra, that's also part of svadhyaya.

Crying to God is meditation

And then the last thing is *ishwara pranidhana* which means, devotion to God. What does Mother have to say about this last one? All the things before this, they are very good. We should do them. But, we're just ordinary human beings. It's very difficult to do what we're talking about. So Mother says, well, don't worry, there's a way out. That's also not easy but it's not so complicated as the other ones. That is *ishwara bhakti*, or ishwara pranidhana; that is devotion to

God. This is the way to control the mind, to get rid of the vasanas. What does Mother say about it?

"*One of the brahmacharis asked Mother, 'Mother, this afternoon you instructed a young man just to pray and cry to God. Is that enough to know God?'*

"*Yes," Mother said, "if performed with all one's heart! Son, don't think that spiritual practice is only sitting in the lotus posture meditating or repeating a mantra. Of course, those two are ways and techniques to remember God and to know the Self. They certainly will help to train and tame the naturally restless body and mind; but it's wrong to think that these practices alone are the way. Take for example the gopis of Vrindavan, or Mirabai. What was their sadhana? How did they become Krishnamayis?—Krishnamayi means one who is full of Krishna—Was it from long hours sitting in meditation?*" (*Were the gopis doing that? Was there time? The gopis were householders.*) "*No. but of course, they did meditate. They did constant and intense meditation but not sitting with crossed legs. Devotees like the gopis and Mirabai constantly remembered the glories of God cherishing His form within themselves irrespective of time or place. They just cried and cried until their tears washed away their entire mind stuff, until all their thoughts were gone.*

"*Children, when we cry, we can forget everything effortlessly. Crying helps us to stop brooding on the past and dreaming about the future. It helps us to be in the present with the Lord and His leela. Suppose someone is very dear to us and they die: say our mother, or father, our husband or our wife, a son or a daughter. We'll lament thinking of him or her, won't we? We forget everything else. At that moment, nothing else comes to mind except the sweet memories of the departed one. We'll have no other interest than thinking about and contemplating that person. Our minds become fully focused. Children, crying has the power to make the mind completely one-pointed. Why do we meditate? To get concentration. So the best way to get concentration is by crying to God. That is a very powerful way of remembering God and that in fact is meditation.*

"That is what great devotees like the gopis and Mirabai did. See how selflessly Mirabai prayed, "Oh, Mira's Giridhari, it doesn't matter if you love me, but Lord, please, don't take away my right to love You!" They prayed and cried until their whole being was transformed into a state of constant prayer. They kept on worshipping the Lord until they were totally consumed by the flames of divine love; they themselves became the offering."

So, this is one way, one easy way for us to meditate; it is to cry to God, or cry to a God-realized person. It doesn't take any special effort to always be thinking of that person, that form, and when we're able to, when we're alone, to cry to them like Mirabai was crying to Krishna. And slowly we'll become full of that Being, and then the vasanas will have no place to exist.

Mother gives the example of a body of salt water. How do you get rid of the salt water? If you go on pouring fresh water into it, more and more and more, it gets diluted until it's virtually not there anymore. So, even though the vasanas are there, we may not be able just to root them out like that. What we can do is put something else in there so there's no space for them anymore. That's the thought of God, or our mantra, or Mother. This is the practical, easy way, for ordinary people like us.

The grace of a *mahatma* also is a saving factor. Mother has something to say about that also:

"Somebody said, 'I've read that no matter how much sadhana one does, the state of perfection can't be reached without the grace of a Realized Guru. Is this true?'"

What do you think? Is this true? Mother said,

"Perfectly correct! In order to remove the subtler vasanas, one needs the Guru's guidance and grace."

It means not just the rough or gross habits that we have, but the subtler things that we're not even aware of.

"And only the Guru can make those things manifest, bring situations that will make those things come out, and then give us the strength to deal with it. And when the vasanas are removed, the last stage, the point when a sadhak falls or glides into the state of perfection cannot happen without the Guru's grace.

"Human beings are limited. Then cannot do much on their own. Maybe they are able to proceed to a certain stage without anybody's guidance or help, but soon the way becomes complex and help is required. The road to liberation is a maze of intricate paths, a labyrinth. In traveling through the maze, a spiritual aspirant may not be able to figure out where to go, or which way to turn. Or following a spiritual path without a Guru can be compared to sailing alone in the ocean in a tiny boat that is not equipped with the necessary equipment, not even a compass to indicate the direction."

That's how hopeless it is if one is trying to realize God

without the help of a God-Realized Master.

"*Remember that the path which leads to the state of Self-realization is very narrow. Two people cannot walk together hand in hand, rubbing each other's shoulders in companionship along this path. One walks this path alone.*

"*As we walk on the spiritual path, there is a light that guides us. That light showing us the path is the Guru's grace. The Guru walks in front shedding light on the path as he slowly and carefully leads us. He knows all the intricate paths by heart. The light of his grace helps us to see and remove the obstacles and reach the ultimate goal.*"

This is what Mother says, that we have to make our effort; that's very important, but ultimately what saves us is the Guru's grace.

"*The Sadguru's grace is what is needed the most. Without his loving care, compassionate glances and affectionate touch, one cannot reach the goal. With each compassionate glance and touch, he is sending forth his grace. Therefore, children, pray for his grace!*"

Namah Shivaya.

Satsang at M.A. Center, 1994
Tape 2 - Side B

Christmas
and the Mystic Christ -1

BEFORE MOTHER CAME TO THIS COUNTRY, or when She was about to come to this country, I had a doubt: how would people react when they saw Mother in Devi Bhava? I thought such a thing has never been, even remotely, seen here. Today I saw something very interesting which clarified a lot for me. I had totally forgotten about this. Today I saw a gentleman sitting in one place, dressed up in an unusual dress, and people came up onto his lap. He gave a hug to each one of them and they told him what their wishes were *(laughter)*. So it's no wonder that the western people could take to Mother like fish to water. Of course, there's a slight difference there.

Today is Christmas Eve, as everybody knows. And, for a spiritual person, the purpose of all these festivals is to increase his or her spirituality. Of course, Christmas has become a time to get together, to be with the family. It's a time for commercialism. It's a time for profit for the businesses. But for us, for devotees, and perhaps the original purpose of Christmas also, was to think about the personality of Christ, who was a great *mahatma*, and to read his teachings and his life.

Why is God so fond of *dharma* ?

No country has a monopoly on sages, mahatmas and ava-tars. Whenever it's necessary, God, the Supreme Being, comes to this earth to bless the living beings. In fact, in the Bhagavad Gita, there's a very famous verse in which Lord Krishna says that when there's a need He comes. Now, what does God consider as a need? Probably all those people that come up to Santa Claus feel that they have a great need that they would like him to fulfill. People that come up to Mother also feel that whatever they need is a real need, very urgent and that God Herself, should fulfill it. But what does God feel is a need? Bhagavan Krishna says that when *dharma* is in decline and *adharma* is increasing, then, as far as He's con-cerned, there's a great need for Him to personally come to this plane of existence.

This is the verse:

"Whenever there is a decay of dharma and an ascendency of irreligion, then I manifest Myself. For the protection of the good, for the destruction of evil doers, for the firm establishment of dharma, I am born in every age."

How is He born? Is He born like us? We're helplessly born in this world according to the fruits of our past actions, our *karma*. Bhagavan, God, is not born in this world like that. He himself says,

"Though I'm unborn, of imperishable nature, and though I'm the Lord of all beings, yet ruling over My own na-ture, I am born by My own maya."

Of His own accord He comes to the world, out of compassion for the individual souls and to upraise or uplift dharma.

Why is God so fond of *dharma?* It must be a very important thing. It's not even that His messengers can do that job. He Himself has to come and uplift *dharma.* So what is the great thing about *dharma?* Well, creation itself is a very mysterious thing. Nobody can say why it is here. The scriptures just say there was one Being alone before creation, *Brahman.* For those of you who don't know it, Brahman comes from the Sanskrit word *brihat* which is great, or vast. That vast Infinity, the Universal Consciousness, That alone existed. Then It thought, "Let Me become many," and the universe came into existence. So this whole universe and all of us are just waves on the ocean of Brahman. The waves aren't different from the ocean, and they don't exist as separate from it. They may have an individual appearance—all of us seem to be individuals, but in the depths we're all one with that Ocean of Intelligence.

So after creation comes into being, then what to do? What's the purpose? Bhagavan says that the world is like a school. Each lifetime is like a class. And the purpose is to graduate and to get your post-graduate degree, that is called *mukti,* liberation, *moksha,* Self-realization, the vision of God. That's the purpose of existence. That's the thing that's driving us on and on, the search for happiness, for bliss, and we can never reach that state of perfect satisfaction until we can merge into the Source, our own Source. That's God or the Self. All the lessons, all the experiences we go through in life are for that purpose, to take us back to the Source. And sometimes the lessons have to be very painful because we have many illusions. We're under illusion all the time, the cosmic illusion, *Maya.* We have to become disillusioned, so that we're going in the right direction, in a one-pointed way. This is the purpose of difficult situations. It is to disillusion us so that we wake up from the dream of *Maya*.

Bhagavan, God, is concerned about His creation. We don't know why it came into existence, but it's here. And the one that created it is concerned about it, like a mother is concerned for her family or children. The scriptures, the sages, the avatars, have come into existence to show us the way to attain the goal of happiness. So this is the importance of dharma, because that is the way. It's not enough just for us to sit and meditate, or to do bhajans or satsang. Spiritual life has to be at every moment of our life, every thought, every word, every action. Then, when we're in tune with dharma, our mind will be in tune with God and we'll achieve the goal of life. We'll become happy. The more we become in tune with dharma, the more our mind will become peaceful and we'll become filled with bliss, or the presence of God. So we have to study, "What is dharma?" We get that from the scriptures, from sages, saints and expecially from the lives of avatars and God-realized souls.

Mother has a very nice thing to say about this, what causes God to come down, or a person who has realized God, what brings them down? Somebody was asking the other day, "Christ was a God-realized person, he was an avatar. When he was on the cross, nailed on the cross, it must have been extremely painful, wasn't it?"

You know, have you ever been pricked by a pin or a thorn? Just a little hole and you're in so much pain. Then what must have been his condition to have spikes nailed through his wrists and his feet? In that condition he said,

"Oh Father, why have you forsaken me?"

After leading a whole life of devotion, surrender, faith, how did those words come out of his mouth at that moment?

The human side of God

Mother gives the answer*,

> "Children, once realization is attained, some beings merge with eternity. Very few of them come down. Who would like to come down after having entered the Ocean of Bliss? In order to come down from that state, that state from which there is no return, it is necessary to have something to hold onto, a determined thought, a sankalpa. Only a few who can make that sankalpa to descend will come down.
>
> "That mental resolve is compassion, love or selfless service to suffering humanity. If you do not want to listen and respond to the call of those sincere seekers, and the cry of those who are suffering in the world, and if you want to remain in the impersonal state and do not want to be compassionate, it is all right. You can remain there.
>
> "When you come down, a curtain which you can pull away at any time, is put up by self-will in order to make functioning in this world more smooth and uninterrupted."

So Mother is speaking, of course, from her own experience. She never read any books. She never met any saints. From her own inner experience she's talking.

> "Consciously you do not pay any attention to the other side of the curtain."

---

*The following quotations are excerpts from Awaken Children 5.

Which side? The side of oneness with God.

"Yet on and off you do go to the other side, but you manage to come back. The very thought or reminder of the other side can simply lift you there. Once you come down then you play the role well."

This is the answer to the question—about Christ—, "you play the role well."

"Once you've come down from oneness with God, you play the role well. You live and work hard for the uplift of all humanity. You'll have problems, obstacles, difficult situations. You'll also have to face abuses, scandals, calumny, but you do not care because although externally you look like everybody else, internally you are different, totally different. Inside you are one with the Supreme Truth. Therefore, you're untouched, unaffected. Having become one with the very source of energy itself, you work tirelessly, healing and soothing the deep wounds of those who come to you. You give peace and happiness to everyone. Your way of living life, your renunciation, love, compassion and selflessness gives inspiration to others to want to experience what you experience. If they do not want to be concerned about the world at all, those compassionate and loving ones who come down can also remain in that non-dual state and merge in Supreme Consciousness. In that state, there is neither love nor lack of love; neither compassion nor lack of compassion.

"In order to express compassion and love, and perform selfless service in order to inspire others to experience those divine qualities, one must have a body. Once

a body is taken, it has to take its natural course. The Mahatma's body is different from an ordinary person's. If he so wills, he can keep the body as long as he wishes without being afflicted by disease and suffering. But he consciously makes the body undergo all experiences that an ordinary human being undergoes. Therein lies his greatness!"

Seeing the life of Christ, or the life of Mother, some people express this doubt:

"If they were divine, if Mother's divine, why does she have to go through so much suffering? Even now, why does she go through so much suffering? "

It's just like when Christ was on the cross and the Pharisees and Saducees came and said, "If you're the Son of God, come down from the cross!" It has nothing to do with being God-realized! God-realization means to be identified with God within, that there's a place within that's unaffected by anything else, even intense pain and suffering. And that place is always calm, never changes. That's the core of their being. But, as Mother says,

"A God-realized soul gives the body to the world, and it goes its natural course. But it can be made to do exceptional things. Didn't Krishna get hurt during the Mahabharata War? Didn't He fight eighteen times with Jarasandha, the powerful and cruel king? Finally, He diplomatically left the battlefield. He could have killed Jarasandha if He wanted to, but Krishna didn't. Remember, it was an arrow shot by an ordinary hunter which put an end to Krishna's life in this world. Jesus was executed on the cross. Both of them could have prevented the events which put an end to their body, but

they let everything happen in the natural course of events.
They let life carry them. They chose to be as they were,
and let the events occur.

"They were willing to surrender. However, this does
not mean that the natural course is inevitable or unavoid-
able for them, as it is for ordinary humans. No, that's
not so. If they had wished, they could have avoided all
bitter experiences. Being all powerful, they could have
effortlessly destroyed those who opposed them, but they
wanted to set an example. They wanted to show the
world that it is possible to live with the highest values of
life even while undergoing all the problems that an ordi-
nary human has. Yet bear in mind that, if a circum-
stance arises where it is necessary for them to break a
law of nature, they can."

So this is what Mother has to say about the nature of a
Realized soul, that they come down through compassion.
They live like ordinary humans in most ways. If necessary,
they can go beyond the laws of nature, as Christ many times
did. All the miracles that he performed, they were not run of
the mill, so to say, happenings. And his words, "Oh Father,
why have you forsaken me?" perhaps it was for those of us
who, in great pain or suffering, also feel that way, that it's
not unforgivable. It's not so bad to feel that way when we're
having so much anguish. Even Christ himself said it. So, he
really showed his humanity, his humanness at that time; it
wasn't due to weakness. It was out of compassion that those
words came out of him. Because, shortly after that, what did
he say?

"Forgive them for they know not what they do."

So it's not that he forgot himself in that moment. Everything is spontaneous and intentional, you could say, from the Divine Will. Whatever comes out of a Divine Person is all for the good of humanity.

Since the purpose of an avatar is to give their teachings to the world, to inspire devotion to their personality as a means of getting devotion, I thought we would read some of Christ's words. I was surprised to find last year that there are many people that have never read anything of the New Testament. In fact, I also had never read the New Testament until I went to India.

Words of Christ

Every word, every single word is a gem. Every word is a spiritual teaching. You could say the gem of the gems, the diamonds are the teachings that he gave his disciples. Because there's the general public, then there's the devotees and then there's the disciples. So the disciples will get the undiluted, distilled truth. And there are many portions in the Bible where he's speaking to the disciples.

This particular version of the Bible that I'm reading is a very American English version. Those of you who've read the King James version, don't be shocked or surprised at this particular version. This is very easy to understand for everybody.

One day, as the crowds were gathering, Christ went up the hillside with his disciples and sat down and taught them there:

"Humble men are very fortunate for the Kingdom of Heaven is given to them."

Now, we should clarify some of our terms here. First of

all, "Kingdom of Heaven," in spiritual life, means God-consciousness. It's not a place off somewhere in some other world or many, many millions and millions and billions of miles beyond the physical universe. The "Kingdom of Heaven," as Christ said, "is within." It's a state of consciousness. When the mind becomes completely calm, then the inner Reality which is hidden by thoughts, starts to shine and one feels one is in heaven. It means one is happy and peaceful. That's heaven. So this is what Christ means when he says "The Kingdom of Heaven."

Also, many times he refers to the Father: "My Father sent me," "I and the Father are one." When he says Father, what he's talking about is Supreme Consciousness, the Absolute Being, Satchitananda, the Ocean of Awareness, the Source of Life, the Source of ourselves, the Source of all our awareness, the Source of the world. That's called the Father. Not that the Father is a man, a big man with a beard, or without a beard. But the Father is Reality, impersonal Reality.

But it's also interesting to note that Mother, when she used to go to school, when she was a little girl—she attended a convent school for some years and she used to sit in the graveyard amongst the tombstones—she said at that time many of the souls that had passed out of their bodies used to come to her. She used to comfort them, and she used to go and see the image of Christ in the chapel. She used to stand there and she would say, "You didn't die. I know that you didn't die!" And she told us that when Christ says, the Father, that he's talking about, however strange it may seem, Shiva. Mother felt that Christ was a devotee of Shiva. Just as Mother is a devotee of Devi and Krishna—even though a person may be a Divine Being, somehow when they come into this world, they also have some object of devotion, either for the sake of others, or it's just inborn in them—so as Mothes' God, you could say, was Krishna and Devi, Mother felt that Shiva was the Lord of Christ.

Now there're many theories that Christ came to India during "the unknown years." You know that the Bible, after he's twelve years old, is silent. It doesn't say anything about where he was until he suddenly reappears when he's about thirty years old. There are many books written that he went to India, he went to Tibet, he went to Egypt, he went to so many places. Well, we really can't prove conclusively anything but, for me, Mother is an authority. She speaks from her own experience and she says that when he says, "Father," he means Shiva.

> *"Those who mourn are fortunate, for they shall be comforted. The meek and the lowly are fortunate for the whole world belongs to them. Happy are those who long to be just and good for they shall be completely satisfied. Happy are the kind and merciful for they shall be shown mercy. Happy those whose hearts are pure for they shall see God."*

This is the most important word in the whole Bible, Old Testament, New Testament, and everything in the Bible: if our mind is pure, we'll see God. If we are not seeing God, we have yet to purify our mind some more. What is meant by purity? Absence of thoughts is purity. The more thoughts that are there the more the mind is lacking in purity. So that the purpose of meditation—that's the purpose of spiritual life—is to reduce the thoughts so that what's real will shine forth.

> *"Happy are those who strive for peace, for they shall*

be called the sons of God. Happy are those who are
persecuted because they're good, for the Kingdom of
Heaven is theirs. When you are reviled and persecuted
and lied about because you are my followers, wonder-
ful! Be happy about it! Be very glad, for a tremendous
reward awaits you. And remember the ancient prophets
were persecuted too."

So unfortunately, the world doesn't understand the
Spirit. The Spirit understands the world. This is, you could
say, the essence of what Christ is saying here. All these qualities are not qualities the people of the world want. The people
of the world don't want to mourn. They don't want to be
meek. They don't want to be forgiving, full of mercy. It's an
aggressive world. It's a competitive world. If you don't get
out there and get what you want, you'll be left behind. That's
the principle of the world. That's the principle of spiritual
ignorance, *maya*. That's not the principle of spirituality, that's
not the principle of God-realized people and *mahatmas*. What
Christ is saying, those are the spiritual principles. They are
hard to practice, especially living in the world. That's the
importance of satsang and reading the scriptures, so that we
do get the right ideas, because the world won't give us the
right ideas.

"Few are the world's seasoning to make it tolerable."

That means the saints, the sages make the world a good
place. Otherwise it's not such a good place.

"If you loose your flavor, what will happen to the
world? Then you yourselves will be thrown out and
trampled underfoot. You are the world's light, a city on

a hill glowing in the night for all to see. Don't hide your light; let it shine for all. Let your good deeds glow for all to see so that they praise your Father.

"Don't misunderstand why I have come. It isn't to cancel the laws of Moses and the warnings of the Prophets. No, I came to fulfill them and to make them all come true. With all the earnestness I have, I say, every law in the book will continue until its purpose is achieved. And so, if anyone breaks the least commandment and teaches others to, he shall be the least in the Kingdom of Heaven. But those who teach God's laws and obey them shall be great in the Kingdom of Heaven."

So, what is he saying here? That spiritual people are really "the salt of the world," they are the essence of the world. They are the ones that make the world a happy place. You know, when we come to Mother, we feel such a happiness, a unique happiness which we don't get through any materialistic means. That is the meaning. In the presence of a spiritual person there's a unique bliss, a happiness which you can't get from the world at all. So they're the salt, they are the essence of the world. And such people, as Mother says, they shouldn't hide themselves. That's exactly what Mother was saying in what we were reading before. That such a person who comes back from Divine Consciousness, they should be compassionate, they should mix with the world. That is the real mahatma!

"Under the laws of Moses, the rule was, 'If you murder, you must die. But I have added to that rule and tell you that if you are only angry, even in your own home, you're in danger of judgment. If you call your friend an

*idiot, you are in danger of being brought before the court.
And, if you curse him, you're in danger of the fire."*

So he's going one step beyond. He's saying, it's not all important that a person does a physical action. Even the small things are important. Even the things we do with our mind are important. So this is a spiritual teaching. It's going deeper; it's subtler.

"If you are standing before the altar in the temple offering a sacrifice to God and suddenly remember that a friend has something against you, leave your sacrifice there, and go and apologize and be reconciled to him and then come and offer your sacrifice to God.

"Come to terms quickly with your enemy before it is too late and he drags you into court.

"The law of Moses says, 'If a man gouges out another's eye, he must pay with his eye. If a tooth gets knocked out, knock out the tooth of the one who did it.' But I say, 'Don't resist violence. If you're slapped on one cheek, turn the other too. If you're ordered to court, and your shirt is taken from you, give your coat too. If the military demand that you carry their gear for a mile, carry it for two. Give to those who ask, and don't turn away from those who want to borrow.

"There is a saying, 'Love your friends and hate your enemies.' But I say, 'Love your enemies. Pray for those who persecute you.' In that way you'll be acting as true sons of God, for He gives His sunlight to both the evil and the good and sends rain on the just and the unjust too. If you love only those who love you, what good is that? Even scoundrels do that much! If you are friendly only to your friends, how are you different from anyone

else? But, you are to be perfect, even as your Father in Heaven is perfect."

That's the goal, that we have to become one with God. Nothing less than that. We have to become perfect. It's quite unimaginable for most of us in our present condition to be perfect. "Be perfect" doesn't mean that we don't make little mistakes when we don't understand things. Perfect means that our conduct, our thoughts, are always in line with *dharma;* that our mind is always in a perfectly pure condition. It's clear like the sky. If we want to think, we can think, but we're not at the mercy of the mind. We can turn it off, or we can use it as we like. In such a mind, everything will be perfect. Perfect knowledge will shine in that mind.

Satsang at M.A. Center, 1994
Tape 3, Side A

Christmas and the Mystic Christ - 2

"Take care! Don't do your good deeds publicly to be admired, for then you will lose the reward. When you give a gift to a beggar, don't shout about it, blowing trumpets in the temple and in the streets to call attention to your charity. I tell you in all earnestness, they have received all the reward they will ever get who do so. But, when you do a kindness to somebody, do it secretly. Don't let your left hand know what your right hand is doing. And your Father, who knows all secrets, will reward you."

SO EVERYONE OF THESE IS A SPIRITUAL TEACHING. In fact, Christ doesn't say anything except purely spiritual words. Some of Christ's teachings are about faith. Some are about devotion. Some are about renunciation. Some are about love. Here's some of his words about renunciation.

St. Francis of Assisi meets the Pope

Many of you might have read about the life of St. Francis of Assisi. He was a real follower of Christ's ideal of renunciation. He felt that, if he was going to be a disciple of Christ, he felt that he should live just the way Christ told in the scriptures, in his life, in his words. We could be a disciple of Christ even today; in fact, that's the whole idea: to become a disciple of a God-realized person, not just to be the devotee— so he was a real disciple of Christ. So, what did he do? He left everything and completely surrendered to the will of God. He led such a simple life! Just the barest necessities; simple food, the most simple dress. Simple means it was more than simple: he used to wear something like a gunny bag!

Today I had to go out somewhere and pass near a place where people were shopping. I felt so strange because, when Christmas time is there, for me, it means thinking about Christ and a life of renunciation. His disciples were walking, not caring about tomorrow or even today, what they'll eat, where they'll sleep, what they'll wear. And here are all these people running about shopping and all the things in the stores which couldn't possibly be necessities. It was such a strange feeling to see that.

And St. Francis, who was really a saint. Mother has a program every year in Assisi, which is just where he was living. His presence is still felt there from him having lived there hundreds of years ago. Amma says that he was the real stuff. That's a very rare comment for Mother to make. She doesn't say that often. Many people ask Mother things about saints and sages and she'll smile or she won't say anything. But to really say such a positive thing is unusual for Mother, unless the person is really an unusual person.

It seems one day St. Francis went to Rome. Why? Because he had built a church with his own hands and with some of his friends and followers. The local bishop and the people who were running the church in the town became very jealous. They came when he was away and burned the church down, and in the process of it one of Francis' brother disciples was killed. So Francis thought that he had done a very bad thing. Perhaps this whole undertaking of his of re-building the old church, even his renunciation and every-thing, maybe was a mistake because one of his brothers had died suddenly like this, in an unnatural way. So he decided to go to the Pope. He thought the Pope must be the repre-sentative of God. He must know everything. He'll certainly be able to tell him whether he's done the right thing or the wrong thing. He went there.

He walked! Now I don't know how far it is from Assisi to Rome. How far is it, anybody knows? It's a long distance barefoot, in a gunny bag, begging his food. It's not like us who'll get in a car, go sixty miles an hour, and stop in the restaurants, and...that's our pilgrimage. No! In the cold, in the rain, barefooted...sometimes they can't reach the next village, no food, two days, three days...

He reached Rome with a number of his brothers, and somehow they got an audience with the Pope—these beg-gars. They were really beggars, but the beggars of God. Those were the disciples of Christ. They were beggars.

They went in there and they saw this unbelievable gran-deur. Have any of you been to the Vatican? I have been there when I was a teenager. It's overwhelming! The grandeur! The beauty! The vastness! The opulence! That's the thing that impressed St. Francis, that's the opulence. He couldn't get over it. He couldn't believe it because it had nothing to do with Christ.

He went in there, and he was looking this side and that side. And there was all the choir and music, and hundreds, thousands of people were there. And the Pope was sitting up at the very pinnacle on a throne. St. Francis started to read some kind of a request which was given to him by somebody else who had arranged this audience. And everybody was look-ing at them and holding their noses, and they thought, "What are these dirty beggars doing here? How did they get in here?" The Pope also was just watching with a skeptical eye.

What happened? Francis couldn't read this concocted document. He threw it down, and he started quoting from the scriptures, from the words of Christ. Here are some of the words, which we were just about to read, but which reminded me of the story:

> *"Don't store up treasures here on earth where they can erode away or may be stolen. Store them in heaven where they will never loose their value and are safe from thieves. If your profits are in heaven, your heart will be there too!"*

So he started to talk like this. And the Pope, I think it was Pope Innocent III—he did have some innocence—and those words pierced his heart; he came down from his throne! When others heard Francis talking like this, they all rushed at him and started shouting, "What an insult! Why is he talking like this? Why is he talking like this! "

These are Christ's words that he is talking! It's not as if it were somebody else's words, or he made it up, or he was abus-ing, or anything. The founder of this vast church—his own words! Well, they didn't understand. They took him and ar-rested him. All the priests were pushing him out the door and then the Pope said,

"Stop! Bring him back!"

They brought him back, and the Pope came over and said, "I was like you when I was young. I was full of earnest-ness to see God, to live the life that Christ told his disciples to live. But somehow or other, I got caught up in all this politics! I'm glad to see your innocence."

What did he do? This is an eighty year old Pope and a twenty year old beggar boy. The Pope got down on his knees, and put his head on Francis' feet and he wept. And other people in the church were thinking,

"Oh God, what's going to happen?"

And one clever man said,

"Don't worry! The Pope knows what he's doing. If he shows this kind of respect to this poor man, he will get all the poor people to again come to the Church."

Of course, that wasn't the Pope's intention. He wasn't that crooked; he was innocent. Then he got up and went back and reluctantly sat on his throne. St. Francis left and went back to his little church in Assisi.

"If your eye is pure, there will be sunshine in your soul. But, if your eye is clouded with evil thoughts and desires, you are in deep spiritual darkness. And oh, how deep that darkness can be!"

Eye? What do you mean, "eye is pure"? Not capital I, e-y-e. "If your eye is pure." It means that whatever the condition of your mind is, that's how you see things through your eyes. If your mind is full of God, you see everything as God. A thief sees everything as an opportunity to steal, a thing to steal. A good person sees everything as a chance to do some good. So everything you see is according to your mental outlook. The eyes are just windows through which everything goes into the mind, and there it's interpreted, something like sun glasses. If you have green sun glasses, everything is green. So, if you have good qualities in your mind, everything is good. Isn't there a saying like that?

Yudhisthira was the oldest son of the Pandavas, the famous Pandavas who are relatives of Sri Krishna. They used to say that there was never an enemy born to Yudhisthira. He had no enemies. Yudhisthira had so many enemies! In fact, this Mahabharata war where there were millions of people killed, all those...half those people, three quarters of those people were Yudhisthira's enemies! They were all out to get him. But the scriptures say, "He had no enemies", because, as far as he was concerned, nobody was his enemy. He saw everybody as his friend. Because his mind was so pure, he never thought of anybody as an enemy, so he had no enemies! He was an innocent. This is called purity of mind, or "a pure eye." Such a person always has the protection of God.

On renunciation and the man
who didn't fear mosquitoes

"You cannot serve two Masters"

This is Christ's teaching about renunciation. That is what we're talking about.

> *"You cannot serve two masters: God and money; for you will hate one and love the other, or else, the other way around. So my counsel is, don't worry about things: food, drink and clothes. For you already have life and a body, and they are far more important than what to eat and what to wear. Look at the birds. They don't worry about what to eat. They don't need to sow, or reap, or store up food, for your Father feeds them. And you are far more valuable to Him than they are.*
>
> *"Will all your worries add a single moment to your life? And why worry about your clothes? Look at the*

lilies of the field; they don't worry about theirs. Yet King Solomon in all his glory was not clothed as beautifully as they are. And, if God cares so wonderfully for flowers that are here today and gone tomorrow, won't he more surely care for you? Oh men of little faith!

So don't worry at all about having enough food and clothing.

"Why be like the heathen, for they take pride in all these things and are deeply concerned about them. But your Father already knows perfectly well that you need them and He will give them to you, if you give Him first place in your life and live as He wants you to."

These are not just words. These words are the experience of every sincere renunciate. It's very difficult to get up that kind of momentum to renounce and to trust in God. But everyone who's done it has experienced the protection of God.

I once knew a person who gave up everything. He had nothing but two pieces of cloth, two *dhotis*, but he had a very big one so he could wrap it around his upper half also. And he had one more, so when he takes a bath he could change it, and then this one he could wash and dry it. He took a vow that he was not going to ask anybody for anything. And he would spend his life walking from one holy place—India is full of holy places, full of temples that have been founded by sages and saints—to another. He decided he was going to spend twenty-five years like this walking from one holy place to another. In each holy place he would do sadhana, meditation, going to the temples, watch the pujas. And he suffered a lot. He walked—never took a vehicle in twenty-five years! He went up into the Himalayas where it's really cold. Can you imagine going outside wearing just a T-shirt and shorts, and sleeping like that outside? For how long? Not just for a few hours...twenty-five years!

I was in the same room as him once, and there were so many mosquitoes in this room at night! I mean.... I've never seen mosquitoes like that. Each one was about this big! And there must have been at least fifteen to twenty thousand mosquitoes in a room this size! It was like Vedic chanting was going on. You've ever heard when many brahmins get together and they chant the Vedas, or when we do bhajans, how loud it is? It was like that—the chanting of the mosquitoes. I couldn't bear it! And somebody gave me a mosquito net. And I covered myself with the net, and I was somewhat peaceful except that there were two or three that got inside the net and they driving me crazy. I was getting very angry! And with the flashlight I was searching for them. I was going to finish them off, these two or three mosquitoes!

And what was he doing? He was laying outside the net on a plank: no blanket, no pillow, no nothing. I had a mattress, a pillow, blanket, everything. All he had was the other cloth that he wears. He just covered himself with it—a thin cotton cloth, like gauze. That was all it was. And he peacefully slept away! He must have been eaten alive! But he didn't care. And then about two o'clock in the morning he got up. He was sitting there in the midst of all the mosquitoes: "Ram! Ram! Ram! Ram!" till six or seven o'clock in the morning. When I looked closely at him in the morning I thought he'd be covered with blood. There was not even a mosquito bite on him. He had so surrendered to the will of God, that God was looking after him. He never starved to death. He was alive after twenty-five years. He was skinny, but skinny doesn't mean weak. He was very strong.

And when he would hear bhajans—this was the beautiful thing—when he would listen to bhajan, he would be in ecstasy. He would get up. He couldn't control himself. He would start to dance and run, shout, scream, laugh. He would fall on the ground, laughing, because he had renounced the thought of everything except God. So when he heard bhajans, that's where his mind would go. He would merge into God and God is bliss. God isn't some somber subject, abstract subject. God is the essence of bliss. So that's what would happen to him. He would get immersed in bliss, in ecstasy.

Christ and the rich man

So the more we have that kind of faith, dependence, renunciation of unnecessary things—doesn't mean that we all have to wander around in *dhotis* for twenty-five years in America, or anything like that. But to minimize, not to have unnecessary things. How many extra pairs of shoes and clothes, and this thing and that thing does each person have? It's unbelievable! Just what is necessary—you have that. And all the rest, give it away. You don't need it. Even money. How much do you need? You keep what you need; the rest, you give it away! This is what Christ was telling when the rich man came to him. Where are those words?

"Someone came to Jesus with this question: 'Good Master, what must I do to have eternal life?'"

Somebody came and said, "What do I have to do to attain Self-realization, liberation, *mukti?*" He shouldn't have asked. (laughter) Don't ask a God-realized person a thing unless you're ready for the answer. Really, seriously. It's better you don't ask if you're not going to follow the advice.

"What do I have to do for eternal life?"

He thought it was going to be something very simple: just go and meditate five minutes, eat vegetarian food, something like that. What does Christ say?

> *"When you call me good,"* (he had said, "Good Master," no?) *"'when you call me good, you're calling me God. For God alone is truly good. But to answer your question, you can get to Heaven if you keep the commandments."*
>
> *"Which ones?"* the man asked.
>
> *Jesus replied, "Don't kill. Don't commit adultery. Don't steal. Don't lie. Honor your father and mother, and love your neighbor as yourself."*
>
> *"I've always obeyed every one of them,"* the youth replied. *"What else must I do?"*

So, he already did all of that, and he still doesn't have eternal life. What is he doing wrong?

> *"Jesus told him—here it goes, 'If you want to be perfect, go and sell everything you have, and give the money to the poor and you'll have treasure in Heaven. And come and follow me.'"*
>
> *"But when the young man heard this, he went away sadly for he was very rich. Then Jesus said to his disciples, 'It is almost impossible for a rich man to get into the Kingdom of Heaven.'"*

It's not that somebody is standing up there at the gate saying, "Are you rich? You can't get in. We let only poor people here. It's just the opposite of earth." No. It means that if the mind is occupied with earthly things, how can you think of God?

Or, if you take it from the point of view of *jnana*, the path of knowledge, if your mind is always outward bent, how can you make it abide in the Self? How can you have that quiet mind that reflects the light of the Self? So a person who's wealthy, ninety-nine percent of the people who are wealthy, they're wealthy because they want to be wealthy. So their minds are occupied with that. Then how can they be thinking of God at the same time? Of course, there'll be a rare group, one percent maybe, who have a lot of money because it was their fate, it happened, but who have no attachment to that. They don't calculate. They just spend according to the need. And they could get up and leave it all in one minute, and never think about it for another second, never turn back and look the other way. So he's saying it's almost impossible for them to get into the Kingdom of Heaven. In other words, it's impossible for them to really meditate deeply.

> *"I say it again, it is easier for a camel to go through the eye of a needle than for a rich man to enter the Kingdom of God."*

This remark confounded the disciples—even the disciples! Not that they were rich. They just thought, "What is he saying? That means that nobody who has any money can get God-consciousness! I don't think they were thinking in terms of God-consciousness themselves. Only afterwards. But they said,

> *"Then who in the world can be saved?" they asked.*
> *Jesus looked at them intently and said, "Humanly speaking, no one. But with God, everything is possible."*

So by God's grace, even somebody who's very attached to wealth can realize Him. Nothing is impossible! In fact, by our own efforts, we're not going to realize God. But we do have to make effort as much as possible, and the rest is left in God's hands.

Christ's most important words

Is there anybody here who doesn't know the story of Christ's life? In brief, after he talked to the disciples and had done various miracles to instill faith into the people, he engaged himself in destroying the evil doers. This was one of his purposes, to purify the society. He was not doing anything to them except destroying the evil in them so that the child in them, the divine child, the innocent child in them could shine forth—just like Mother does. In those days, the Pharisees and Sadducees, the priests, were supposed to be the people who were to show the public the way to realize God, the path to God. But they didn't care either about that or anything else truly religious. They were caring more about business. This is what Christ says,

"You've turned this temple into a market place!"

He went in there and he started knocking things down left and right. He's saying,

"This is a den of thieves...!"

And it was all run by the priests in those days! All these people, because they didn't have any truth in them, couldn't accept his words, and finally they plotted against him, and brought him to court. He was tried, convicted and executed.

He was crucified.

It seems that long before this, there were many mahat-mas in Israel that had said at various points of time that things like this would happen. They said that somebody would be coming, an avatar. They call him the Messiah. And he would be the fruit of all the years, of all the spiritual life and the religious life and the dharmic life of all the people before his birth. It was all told what would happen, even the words that he would speak. And when they asked him, "Are you this one?" He said, "I'm that one."

Even that, they couldn't swallow, they couldn't accept. So he was ultimately crucified. And at the end he said:

> *"Father, forgive them for they know not what they do."*

Mother's saying that this has to be our attitude; that we have to get those qualities. Even they had the power to rec-tify the situation. They had the power to protect themselves, but they didn't. On the other hand, they stressed on forgive-ness, mercy, compassion.

So the last thing that Christ has said was really the best thing that he could say. It was really the thing that he had to say. And it's the thing that we have to remember because it's not only true of Christ, it's true of any avatar, any divine being. It's that thing which gives us the strength to go on. It's that thing which gives us the comfort, the consolation and the faith that whatever may come, our avatar, our God is with us.

After he got killed, after three days, he resuscitated his body; he brought it back to life, and that's child's play for such a person. He came to his disciples, his children, and he talked with them and just before he left, this is what he said:

"Be sure of this, that I am with you always even to the end of the world."

Namah Shivaya.

Satsang at M.A.Center, 1994
Tape 3 - Side B

Detachment - 1

WE HAVE BEEN READING THE OMKARA DIVYA PORULE song of Mother's which is concerned with the *Vedanta* or *Advaita* philosophy, that is, that you are the *Atma*, you are not the body, that the body dies but not you and that the bliss that you seek all the time, every day, every moment of your life is not outside of you but it is that *Atma*, your real Self.

Mother has not herself written any of these verses, but it is rather what she has said, her teachings, and one of the *brahmacharis* wrote it down in the form of a song.

There is one verse, which we discussed last time. I'll read it:

Tyagam manassil varanyal kurum tapam varum mayamulam
A satiraikiloklesam varum sarva nasam varum buvil arkum

That means, if the mind is devoid of renunciation, great suffering will befall one through *maya*, illusion. If desire is not uprooted, affliction follows, which will culminate in the utter ruin of anyone in this world.

Story of Bhartrihari

When we were discussing this verse, I was telling the story about a mahatma named Bhartrihari, how he was a king. He was a great devotee, but he was a king. He was not a monk or a renunciate. A sage came to him and gave him a fruit, saying that, "If you eat this fruit, you will become immortal, or you will live a very long time." Then the king gave the fruit to the queen who was his favorite and finally the fruit came back to him through so many turns of having become a gift to somebody else. The queen gave it to her boyfriend. Her boyfriend gave it to his girlfriend. His girlfriend gave it to her boyfriend. Like that, it went and it finally ended up somewhere out in the city with somebody. That person felt that they weren't fit for such a thing, and that the king was the most fit person for this wonderful fruit. They came and gave it to the king. The king traced the whole thing out and found out that his wife was not faithful to him.

That realization—that what he thought was the dearest thing to him, that means his wife—that she wasn't even faithful to him, that her so-called love was so shallow—that woke him up from the sleep of *maya*. He started thinking more serious things. He decided to leave the world in which he had spent his whole life seeking dreams. He became a *sannyasi*, a monk and he went to a cave, I believe it was somewhere in Bihar. He did tapas the rest of his life. And he wrote these hundred verses of renunciation.

They are called the *Vairagya Satakam* and are in Sanskrit. It's superb. There's probably no book written on detachment or renunciation like this one. The closest thing you could say that's there in traditional literature is *Bhajagovindam* by Sankaracharya, which also is concerned with the same topic of the transitoriness of the world, the illusory nature of worldly happiness, and the greatness of Self-realization.

So, we are going to read some of the verses from the *Vairagya Satakam* because it's not a divergence from Mother's teaching at all. It's an expansion, you could say.

Why does Mother stress so much on renunciation? As we've talked so many times, renunciation does not mean becoming a sannyasi and going off into the woods or living in an ashram and doing tapas. Everybody has to practice a certain amount of renunciation, even in their daily life.

Suppose you come home from school. Tomorrow you have an exam, a test, but your mind says, "I want to watch the TV." Your intellect says, "No, no, I've got to do my homework or I'm gonna flunk the test." What are you going to do? Are you going to follow what your mind and senses say or are you going to follow what your intellect says? Ashok, are you going to run for the computer games, or are you going to do your studying?

—Computer work.

—Right. Why?

—Because otherwise I'll flunk the test.

—Right. That's going to cause you big trouble if you flunk the test. So you put the temporary pleasure aside and you go for the long-term improvement, betterment. Right? That's called renunciation.

We're all doing that.

Anybody who is doing anything in this world, if they want to succeed, they have to do a certain amount of control of their mind and senses, because the very nature of the mind and senses is to wander. It's natural that we feel that happiness is outside in the sense objects, that's everybody's experience; but, if we just let our senses run wild and do whatever they want, that will just destroy us. We will have no concentration. We won't be able to do anything. We'll end up in a pit. The Upanishads give the example of a person driving a chariot and holding onto the horse's reins. If you just let go of the reins and let the horse run, what's going to happen?

It's going to go off into the pit. Then you are going to get hurt. So you have to learn how to hold the reins and control the horses. Our senses are just like that. If we don't learn that, then we have to suffer. It doesn't matter who we are. We can't say, "I didn't know."

It's just like fire. Suppose there's a gas stove and it's burning, and you don't know what fire is. You never saw it. You are very little. you're only one year old or something. You say, "Oh, it's so nice! It's so pretty!" And you stick your finger in that. What's going to happen? It's going to get burnt. Can't you tell the fire, "I'm just a little girl? I didn't know you were going to burn me. You shouldn't have burned me." Can you say that? You can say that. Fire is not going to care about you. The laws of nature are such that they don't care who goes against them. They don't care how innocent you are, or how ignorant you are. Those are the laws. So the senses, they don't care anything about us, they have their own nature, the mind has its own nature. But we, the soul, the Atman, have to learn how to control them if we want to have a peaceful existence, if we want to lead a proper life, not a scattered life.

Mother says that this self-control can be taken to the extreme, that the mind can become so under control and so calm that we can attain the state of Self-knowledge. That's the criteria for realizing the presence of God if you take it from the viewpoint of *bhakti*, devotion. Or if you want to experience who you are, that you are really the immortal Atman and not the body, then also the mind has to become completely calm so that experience can arise. This outward tendency of the mind has to be curbed, both for worldly improvement and spiritual realization.

Story of Parikshit and the Srimad Bhagavatam

Many of you might have read the *Srimad Bhagavatam*. That's many stories of Sri Krishna's life and many of the incarnations of Lord Vishnu, the lives of many devotees of Lord Vishnu, many kings. It's a history. It has so many lessons. It's being told to a king named Parikshit who was going to die within one week. He had seven days to live. He came to know that in seven days he was going to die. It was his fate that he was going to be bit by a very poisonous snake, and definitely he was going to die. When he heard that news, he saw life in a totally different way. Until then he was having a very good time. He was a good king, but he was also just having a good time like everybody else tries to have in the world, but when he heard that he's going to die in one week for sure, without fail, everything changed. He realized, "What was the use of everything that I did in my life? What's the use of my kingdom, my family, my wealth, my prestige, my everything, my health? It's all going to go down the drain in one week. Isn't there something more lasting than this?"

Because he was a spiritual person, he knew that there is something more worthwhile than the passing things of the world—that is the Self, the *Atman*, the vision of God. So he sat down by the side of the Ganges River and started to meditate. Why? Do you know why we meditate? Because our mind is so restless that we have to somehow calm it down to get that inner vision. One of the processes is meditation. When you reach that stage where you want to see what's inside you, you want to experience peace, then you feel that the sense world becomes a great distraction for you. Many people reach that stage. From there, what do they do? They learn the spiritual practices. You start to feel the stress that the senses are putting on you—all five of them are running in all five directions. They always want their stimulus and their satisfaction. Some people—having experienced everything they wanted through their senses and they still didn't get the satisfaction—they realize, "What a terrible thing this is! My senses are pulling me apart! Even though I don't want it, they are persisting." That's called vasana.

Mother gives an example of what is meant by vasana. We make a decision, "I'm not going to do that anymore," then the past habit makes us do it again. She gives the example of the dog and the jackal. Whenever the jackal would go by, the dog would start barking. Then the dog decided, "I'm not going to waste my time like this. Why should I bark at the jackal?" The next time the jackal went by, sure enough, the dog started barking again.

Or the cat—she gives another nice one about the cat who wanted to learn how to read and write. Did you ever hear about that cat? No? There was a cat that got fed up with catching mice. It said, "There must be a better way to make a living than always running after mice. Suppose I learn how to read and write. I could probably get some employment, temporary of course." So the cat got a correspondence course and it was having a book. It use to sit up at night with a candle and it would read the lessons. Everything was going on okay for about a week. Then one night, a mouse ran by. The cat just knocked over the candle, went running after the mouse, forgot all its lessons. That's vasana. We make a decision: "I'm not going to do this thing anymore—whatever it may be." Then when the situation comes in front of us, again we do it. That's vasana. This is another reason for trying to cultivate self-control and renunciation, so that we don't have to dance to the tune of our senses and our habits.

So this king was trying to meditate, but he couldn't. When you are very thirsty for the state of inner peace, for whatever cause—either you suffered a lot or you had a glimpse of some spiritual state or you met a mahatma like Mother—whatever the reason is, when you really get thirsty for that, then your teacher comes. You don't even have to go looking for a master or a guru. It will happen. That meeting has to happen. That's the law of nature, spiritual law.

When Parikshit was sitting there struggling and meditating, Suka (he was a great, realized soul) came there. Not only him, so many mahatmas came with him. He was going to initiate Parikshit in a very unique way: he told him a long story. It took him seven days to tell the story. That was the *Srimad Bhagavatam*. And at the very end, Suka says, "I told this whole thing about the nature of the universe and what spiritual life is all about and devotion and meditation and wisdom and detachment and all that, only for one reason: just so that you would get a feeling of dispassion towards the sense objects. Because only if that dawns on you will you be able to experience the peace and bliss of your soul, the Atman.

Through a mixture of devotion—because he heard all these stories about Krishna's life and all the avatars of Vishnu—and through the imminence of death—so he was serious about it—and through having the nature of the world revealed to him through the words of Suka, he finally closed his eyes after seven days of hearing *Bhagavatam* and he tore the veil of illusion, meaning his mind came to a perfect standstill, it stopped. In that still mind, he saw himself, his real Self. He lost all body-consciousness, world consciousness. If you have no body-consciousness, you have no world consciousness either. Just as in sleep, if you lose your body consciousness, there's no world either for you. He lost all external consciousness, but he was fully conscious within of his real Self. In that state, the snake came and it bit him and his body died. But he was forever merged in the bliss of the Atman.

Words of Bhartrihari on desire and renunciation

Renunciation—in the sense of being able to turn off the mind, to turn off the senses and to keep perfectly still, trying to get the inner vision—is very necessary. This we get through satsang, through a person's presence like Mother, or through the stories of the scriptures. So this *Vairagya Satakam* was written for that purpose. Of course, it must have been written by Bhartrihari out of his experience, but it was also written for the good of others.

We will read as much of it as we can in the time that we have.

"All glory to Shiva, the Light of Knowledge, residing in the temple of the yogi's heart, who smites away like the rising sun, the massive front of the endless night of ignorance, overcasting the human mind, in whose wake follows all auspiciousness and prosperity, who burnt up Cupid as a moth as if in sport, and who appears beaming with the rays of the crescent moon adorning His forehead."

Bhartrihari's *ishta devata*, his god, was Lord Shiva, so he's starting his work with a prayer to Shiva. He's praising Shiva. I'm not going to read every single verse. It's a hundred verses, and I'm only going to read about thirty of them.

"The worldly pleasures have not been enjoyed by us, but we ourselves have been devoured."

Have you ever eaten too much? The food looked so delicious. You enjoyed it, but you couldn't stop eating. What happened? What started out as a pleasure ended up as a pain. Right? Ended up as a tummy-ache. That's what the senses do. Moderation is okay, but if you don't control the accelerator, so to say, then instead of you eating them, they'll eat you.

"No religious austerities have been gone through, but we ourselves have become scorched. Time is not gone, but it is we who are gone because of the approach of death. Desire is not reduced in force, even though we ourselves are reduced to senility."

So Mother says that desire—however old the person is, you may be a hundred years old—desire is always sixteen years old. Just because you see an old person, don't think that they don't have any desires. Their desires are just as strong as a sixteen-year-old youth.

"The face has been attacked with wrinkles. The head has been painted white with gray hair. The limbs are enfeebled, but desire alone is rejuvenating."

The body is falling apart, but the desire is not getting any weaker, because it can't—that's its nature. Unless you do something about it, it's not going to get weaker with age. Don't think like this: "Oh, when I'm eighty years old, I'm going to stop all these things and I'm going to meditate and I'm going to go to an ashram." Don't think like that. Desire is not going to stop and it is desire that makes the mind and senses restless, but it's not such an abstract thing as we may think. Even though it has no form, we know what it is. We know what it does at least. It's that thing that makes our mind run outward, that force.

> *"Though my friends, dear to me as life, have all taken such a speedy flight to heaven,"* (means my friends died) *"though the impulse for enjoyment is wearied out, and the respect commanded from all persons lost, though my sight is obstructed by cataracts and the body can raise itself but slowly on a staff, still—alas for its silliness— this body startles at the thought of dissolution by death."*

So even though I'm falling apart, all my friends died, my body is falling apart, I'm so old I can hardly get up with a stick, still when I think of death, I shake.

> *"Hope is like a flowing river, of which the ceaseless desires constitute the waters. It rages with the waves of longing, the attachments for various objects are its animals of prey. Scheming thoughts are the birds, and it destroys in its course the big trees of patience and fortitude. It is rendered impassable by whirlpools of ignorance and of profound depth. As it is, its banks of anxious deliberation are precipitous indeed. Such a river the great yogis of pure mind pass across to enjoy supreme bliss."*

Hope—that means we get a desire, then next thing that comes is hope, that we will be able to fulfill the desire. This whole thing is the working of *maya*. That's what the scriptures say and that's what Mother says. All sages and saints say the same thing. This whole idea that we are going to be permanently happy through something or other outside of ourselves is due to the cosmic illusion that's called maya.

Our whole spiritual life is only trying to go beyond the force of maya. If you want to shoot up in the sky, you want to go beyond the force of gravity, what do you have to do? If you just sit here, it's not going to just disappear. Suppose you want to fly. What do you have to do? You have to go in an airplane. Why an airplane? Suppose you want to go beyond the air, then what do you need? Spaceship. Then what does the spaceship do? It has to go a certain speed, doesn't it? Then when it reaches a certain velocity of escape, then it's free of—what's that force called? Gravity, right. So you could sit here on earth forever. Gravity is not going to let go. That's its nature: similarly maya, it's never going to let us go. It's not that it's cruel or that it's wicked or that it's a bad joke. It's just its nature, just like fire. Fire is not cruel. It has its purpose. Can you imagine if there was no gravity? What would be going on? We would all be floating around in the room. We would be hitting each other, and all kinds of things would be going on. Gravity is necessary. But if we want to go beyond it for some reason, we need the velocity of escape. We have to reach a certain point where we're free of it. Then it's all free fall or free flying.

If we want to escape from the force of maya, if we don't want to dance to the tune of what our senses always tell us, if we want to be free of the illusion that happiness is possible through any temporary thing, we have to fight. We have to fight as long as necessary until we have escaped the force of maya. That's called *moksha* or liberation or Self-realization. How much do we have to fight? How frequently do we have to fight? It's like saying, "How frequently do I have to fly to get beyond gravity?" You have to fly until you're beyond gravity.

This is the importance of constant effort in spiritual life, constantly reminding yourself of these things. This is why even though you are coming here every week, I am saying the same things again and again and again. It's not that I have gone beyond maya. It's for myself also. It's refreshing my memory. Every time I read something like this, every time I hear myself saying it, it's waking me up to the truth that maya is always trying to pull me down and that I should try to wake up. So these things, they shake us, they wake us up, that the body is going to die. Even though it is getting older, still the desires are not getting less. I haven't been happy, whatever I might have done in this world. Whatever peace and bliss I achieved, it was only when I improved my meditation or my self-control. So these are the means: these words.

> *"The objects of enjoyment, even after staying with us for a long time, are sure to leave us some time. Then what difference does their privation in this way make to men, that they do not of their own accord discard them?"*

We were talking about this the other day. There's this saying that "You can't take it with you." Well, there is one way you can take it with you. How can you take it with you? Do you know that saying? —"You can't take it with you." Ashok, do you know that one? No? That means when you die, you can't take anything with you. You leave everything here. So how do you take it with you? There's a way to take it with you. You know how to take it with you?
—God-realization.
—Of course, that's the highest, but even before we attain God-realization. It's a secret. It's a trick. It's very secretive. If you want to take something with you, suppose you've got a thousand dollars you want to take with you. No, I'm not joking! You've got a thousand dollars, you want to take

it with you. What you should do is, you should give it to somebody. Give it away, because whatever you give away, that's what you're going to take with you. Does that make sense? Because that's the law of *karma*: whatever you do, you'll get back. The only way of taking things with you is by giving them away. Then, at the right moment, they'll be there for you. Strange, huh? But that's it.

So what he's saying here is, even though we know that we can't hold on to the objects of our enjoyment, that either they are going to leave us or we are going to leave them, why is it that we can't give them away before that? If enjoyments leave us of their own initiative, if they tear themselves away from us, they produce great affliction of mind. Suppose somebody steals something from you, or suppose there's a disaster in your business—something's lost, everything's lost—you feel miserable, but it's not the same if you had given that thing away. Then you feel happy. If men voluntarily renounce these objects, they conduce to the eternal bliss of Self-realization. You don't want to give in order to get, that's not the idea; that's not the principle we are trying to learn here. That's business. But if you give, then you don't want to get anymore and you're happy. It's the wanting to get, the desire, that makes us miserable, makes us mean, makes us restless. When you don't want to get anymore and you want only to give, then what you get is something quite different than what you give. You get the state of peace. Nothing else can give that except renunciation.

"Blessed are those who live in mountain caves meditating on Brahman, the Supreme Light, while birds devoid of fear perch of their laps and drink the teardrops of bliss that they shed in meditation. While our life is fast ebbing away in the excitement of revelry in palatial man-

sions or on the banks of refreshing pools or in pleasure gardens, all created and brooded over merely by imagination."

So, blessed are those who live in the bliss of meditation on God and who shed tears of bliss, and the birds sit on the laps of such people because they have no fear of them.

"For food I have what begging brings, and that too tasteless, and once a day. For a bed, the earth. For an attendant, my body itself. For dress, I have a worn-out blanket made up of a hundred patches and still, alas! the desires do not leave me."

Even though I have nothing, I have renounced everything, I am unable to renounce desire. Such a strong thing desire is!

"Without knowing its burning power, the insect jumps into the glowing fire."

Have you ever seen that? A moth fly into a fire? Fly into a light bulb? Well, it would do that into a fire if it could find a fire.

"The fish, through ignorance, eats the bait attached to the hook, whereas we, having full discernment, do not renounce the sensual desires, complicated as they are with manifold dangers. Alas, how inscrutable is the power of delusion!"

Just want to remind you that neither Mother nor the scriptures nor anybody is saying that everybody should become a yogi in the cave or that nobody should go for a worldly life and have a good time. That's not it, but one should have this knowledge also, by the side. Keep this in your back pocket, because if at some time in your life, you find that it didn't work, that your search for happiness through sense-happiness or through worldly life didn't work, that it didn't fulfill your urge, then you'll have something to fall back on, you'll remember these words. And then you can go for something else, which is called spiritual life or divine bliss.

> "When the mouth is parched with thirst, man takes cold refreshments. When suffering from hunger, he swallows cooked rice made delicious. When set on fire by lust, he embraces his partner. So happiness is but the remedy of these diseases, of hunger, thirst, and lust. And behold, how man is upset in its quest!"

He's comparing the thirst of the senses to a kind of disease. This is one way to think of it. Our senses get restless, they get stimulated, they get agitated, and then to get rid of that irritation, so to say, we do various things. This is what our life is like.

> "Possessed of tall mansions, of sons esteemed by the learned, of untold wealth, of a beloved wife, and thinking this world to be permanent, men deluded by ignorance run into this prison-house of the world, whereas blessed indeed is he who, considering the transience of the same world, renounces it. The pit of our stomach is so hard to fill, and it is the root of no small undoing."

Why does he say that? Because if you didn't have to eat every day, you'd have a lot less problems. Apart from indigestion, overweight, and all these things, you wouldn't have to get a job if you had a simple life because you wouldn't have to eat. You have to eat because you have to live. So if you were able to live under a tree with a minimal amount of clothing, that would be enough. You wouldn't need anything else, but if you have to eat, you need money, you need so many things.

> *"It is ingenious in severing the vital knots as it were of our fond self-respect."*

What's that? Our stomach. Many people will throw away all their self-respect in order to be able to satisfy the stomach.

> *"It is like the bright moonlight shining on the lotus that blooms only in the sun. It is the hatchet that hews down the luxuriant creepers of our great modesty."*

> *"In enjoyment, there is the fear of disease."*

Because if you are sick, you can't enjoy properly. Suppose you like to eat but you don't have a good stomach or you don't have teeth, so you can't enjoy. Suppose you like to see nice things, but your eyes don't work properly. Suppose you like to hear sweet music, but you are hard of hearing. So if you have any kind of disease, enjoyment is a problem. It could also mean that the loss of energy that is used during enjoyment may result in illness.

> *"In social position, there's the fear of falling off if your happiness depends on social position. In wealth, there's the fear of thieves; in honor, the fear of humilia-*

tion; in power, the fear of foes; in beauty, the fear of old age; in the body, the fear of death.

"All the things of this world pertaining to man are attended with fear. Renunciation alone stands for fearlessness. Health of men is destroyed by hundreds of ailments of the body and mind. Wherever there is Lakshmi, there, perils find an open access."

Now what's meant by this? Lakshmi means the goddess of wealth, prosperity. So wherever there is prosperity, the sages say that it is an open door to misery because prosperity has so many complications. Most people in this world don't think in this way. "If there's prosperity, there's happiness; all our worries are over" is the normal way of thinking, but a real spiritual person won't care a fig for prosperity. Their wealth will be the wealth of inner peace.

Story of Lakshmi who appears to Swami Vidyaranya

You might have heard the story of Swami Vidyaranya. He was the Prime Minister of king Krishnadevaraya, a famous king. He built the Vijayanagar kingdom. This Prime Minister had a desire to be prosperous and wealthy like everybody else does, so he did all the pujas to Lakshmi. He did them three times a day. He did ten thousand mantras. He used to do japa, Lakshmi's mantra. Day and night, he went to the Lakshmi temples. He did so many vows in order to get Lakshmi's grace so that he would become wealthy. He went on like this for years and he didn't become wealthy. He got fed up and realized, "Why am I giving so much energy for this? My life is ebbing away." He decided he's going to become a sannyasi and try to realize God, attain immortality,

Self-realization. So he left the house. He put on his sannyasi's clothes, the ochre cloth, and just then this beautiful lady appeared before him. Well, you know who that was— Lakshmi! Then he said, "Can I do something for You?"

She said, "You've been praying to Me all these years. Now I have finally come."

He said, "Now You come and now I don't want You."

Then She said, "I have to give you something."

Then he said, "Okay, give me the wealth of spiritual knowledge. Give me the wealth of Realization." So She blessed him, that he would be a wise man full of scriptural knowledge and spiritual experience. Then got the name Vidyaranya because of the blessings of Lakshmi. "Vidyaranya" means one who is a forest of learning, so wise.

So seeking Lakshmi for wealth will end up at a dead-end ultimately, because of all the problems that we've been discussing here: death, enemies, thieves, and all the things that the world is made of.

"Whatever is born, dies."

Then what is created as stable by the creator? There's nothing stable in this world.

"Enjoyments of embodied beings are fleeting, like lightning in the clouds. Life is insecure as a drop of water on a lotus leaf. The desires of youth are unsteady. Realizing this quickly let the wise firmly fix their minds in yoga, easily attainable by patience and equanimity. Old age looms ahead, frightening men like a tiger. Diseases afflict the body like enemies. Life is flowing away like water running out of a leaky vessel. Still, how wonderful that man goes on doing wicked deeds!"

We're only about half way through and it is already getting pretty late. We'll continue and try to finish it next week.

Namah Shivaya

Satsang at M.A. Center, 1994
Tape 4 - Side A

Detachment - 2

WE'VE BEEN TALKING ABOUT SOME OF MOTHER'S VERSES in *Omkara divya porule*, Mother's Vedantic verses, the verses on the philosophy of Vedanta or Advaita, that is non-dualism, that you yourself are the Self, not the body, and that unfortunately, all of us are asleep, deep asleep in the dream world called maya or universal illusion and the only way to wake up is through intense spiritual practice and detachment from the dream.

We started this discussion a couple weeks ago. I just want to stress at the beginning that this isn't the only teaching of Mother's. Mother also teaches that through intense devotion to God, through surrender to God, through various devotional paths or through the path of selfless service, also the mind can wake up to its true nature, which is the Atman, the immortal Self; but because we started with the *Omkara divya porule*, now we are talking about the non-dual philosophy and the need for vairagya. I'll explain what I mean by vairagya in a second.

When we say that we are asleep in maya, "maya" means that force which makes us forget reality, which is always there and makes us take what's in front of us as reality and then gets us into trouble. Not only do we forget reality, we forget even realities. Suppose there's a very little boy, one and half, two years old. Before he knows anything about this world, you put some gold coins in front of the little boy and you also put some cookies in front of him. Which one do you think the little boy is going to take? Cookies. Unanimous? Yes. Cookies. Why? Why the cookies? Tangible, right. Also the little boy doesn't know that with the gold coins, he could buy mountains of cookies. He sees only the immediate pleasure that is right there in front of him. He is not thinking about long-term investments, or anything like that. So, this is what maya is: all the time, we see the immediate pleasure, the immediate happiness that a thing gives us; we go for it and we ignore everything else, the long-term truth.

So we're talking about vairagya, how to wake up from this maya. Mother says that vairagya is the essential thing. Even Sankaracharya—you might have heard of him—he also says that you could have no other good quality except, and that would be enough for you to attain Self-realization or to go beyond the cycle of birth and death. So what is this vairagya? Vairagya means lack of, or the absence of *raga*. That means a lot? No. Raga is not only that thing that you play the music to, which is a tune; but *raga* means attraction or attachment to a thing. Our mind is always going between either attraction towards this and that or repulsion towards this and that, and sometimes indifference also is there. So, lack of attraction or lack of attachment is vairagya. This is the thing that will wake us up from the dream. It's because of our attachment or because of our attraction towards the dream of maya that we stay asleep. That generates a certain momentum and a certain energy and it perpetuates itself in births and births and births. It becomes very complicated, because as long as we're asleep, the law of karma holds true. Everything that we do in this dream has its action and reaction. The only way we can break this wheel or break this cycle is to wake up. That means we have to withdraw our mind from the dream, and then it will break. When we break the dream, then that's called *bhoda* or enlightenment or Self-realization or liberation from the cycle of birth and death, *mukti* or *moksha*. I'll give you a concrete example of what is vairagya.

Story of Samarta Ramdas and the kingdom of Shivaji

There used to be a great mahatma named Samarta Ramdas. You might have heard of him. He lived four or five hundred years ago in India. He was a sannyasi. He wasn't always a sannyasi but he had the makings of a sannyasi. He was a great devotee of Hanuman. That was his favorite aspect of God. He emulated all the qualities that Hanuman had: devotion to Ram and service and renunciation.

Actually, he was about to get married. In the marriages in India—I don't know if it's still done like this, but in those days it was very orthodox—the boy and the girl, they'd sit facing each other and there would be a screen between them, kind of like a piece of cloth or a curtain. Just before they're about to meet and get married, the priest says, "Be alert! *Jagrata!*" So, when Ramdas heard the "Jagrata! Be alert!", somehow, because he was destined to become a sannyasi, immediately it flashed in his mind, "I'd better be alert! Am I sure I want to get into this complicated situation? Have I understood all the implications? Is everything going to be all right?" So that one word, "Be alert," brought all these thoughts up in his mind, and he jumped like a monkey, he jumped off the seat, ran out of the marriage hall, and nobody saw him for the next twelve years. This is called real detachment, but it didn't end there.

(Voice from the audience) "Probably he was real scared."

Well, it may start out as fear of suffering and complications and all these things, but not everybody feels that way. Not everybody has to run away to the forest for twelve years, but he was destined to become a monk, so it happened like that. One word was enough. Nobody had to explain all these things to him again and again. He didn't have to read any books. He wasn't calculating, "Well, if I do this, what's going to happen? If I do that, what's going to happen? Should I do this or should I do that?" No.

So, he jumped, he ran, and he started doing intense spiritual practices in the forest. They found him standing in the river up to his neck in cold water in the winter time in north India where it gets down to freezing. He used to stand the whole day and night, sometimes for days together, doing his *mantra japa.* He used to stand in the hot sun with fire burning around him, all these kinds of severe penance, to become what?—more detached from his physical existence and from the world and to be merged in the Self, the soul.

He finally attained perfection through his sadhana. One day, he was walking through one of the towns and the king of the town, Shivaji, was having his palace there. Ramdas just walked by the palace. He was begging. He had his begging bowl, a coconut shell that was hollowed out and all cleaned up. He was going up to each house and saying, *"Biksham dehi ca Parvati,"* "Oh, Divine Mother, please give me alms." He came to the gates of the palace and Shivaji came running out. Ramdas held out his bowl. The Guru held out a bowl to the disciple. Ramdas said, "Please give me alms." Shivaji took out a pen and a paper, wrote down something, and put the paper in the bowl. Ramdas said, "What kind of nonsense is this? Is this paper going to satisfy my hunger?"

Then Shivaji said, "Please, read the paper, Swamiji."

So he took the paper out of the bowl. He looked at the paper. What was the paper? Shivaji had signed over the entire kingdom to Ramdas. The entire kingdom!

He said, "The whole thing is yours. I don't want any more to do with the kingdom. This is my alms to my Guru." It's not unbelievable. There are people who do that even today. So much devotion they have in their Guru, so much love for their Guru, so much they are fed up with the world, and so much faith, and so they just give—everything, not just their time, not just their mind, not just their heart, even their possessions—everything, without calculating, everything they give to their Guru. Fearless, like jumping off a cliff, not knowing what's going to happen and just before you reach the ground, something catches you and softly places you on the ground.

So, Shivaji gave the whole kingdom to Ramdas. He read the note and said, "Thank you very much, but you keep it in trust for me. You look after it. It's mine now: you look after it for me." He left for the next house for his *biksha*, for his alms. This is real vairagya, for both of them. This was double vairagya. The disciple had real detachment; the Guru had real detachment. Nobody wanted the kingdom.

This is a practical example of what is vairagya. This is what is needed to make the mind steady. It's lack of vairagya, lack of detachment that makes our mind so restless. It's always running after one thing or another. If it gets one thing, it stops running for about a second or two. Then again, a new thing comes up in the mind. It wants to run after something else. It never stands still more than a second or two except when? —When we go to sleep or when we are in *samadhi*. Most of us have never been in samadhi, so it's mostly when we're in sleep.

This constant restlessness, eventually we get fed up with it. At that stage, you could say, we are on our way back to the real Self. We're on our way back to God. We have to reach that stage where we say, "Oh, I've had enough of this endless restlessness. Whatever I've gotten, whatever I've done, I still didn't get that peace. I get it and it goes away. I get it and it goes away."

There's a very nice verse written by one saint. He's describing this nature of how we have to go back to the Self or we have to ultimately get back to God, that we can't help it. That's the very nature of things: that everybody will have to reach that stage. They will reach that stage of real vairagya. Here's the verse. It's very nice.

> *"The waters rise up from the sea as clouds, then fall as rain and run back to the sea in streams. Nothing can keep them from returning to their source. Likewise, the soul rises up from Thee and cannot be kept from joining Thee again although it turns in many eddies on its way. A bird which rises from the earth and soars into the sky can find no place of rest in mid-air, but must return again to earth. So indeed must all retrace their path, and when the soul finds the way back to its source, it will sink and be merged in Thee, O Ocean of Bliss!"*

This is what happens to us. We are like the water that's risen up from the sea, and we fall down on the earth, and we become a river that goes in so many ways, this way and that way, and finally we get back to the sea... or like a bird that rises up: it has to come down. It cannot live up in the air. It gets exhausted.

Where is the goal? Where is the source? It's the Ocean of Bliss: that's the thing we're looking for all the time, but we always miss it.

The verses of Bhartrihari

We were talking about *Vairagya Satakam*, which is probably the greatest of the writings of saints about this science of detachment. We started reading that the other week and I wanted to continue and maybe even finish it today because every verse in that is so awakening. It really shakes us. It touches something in us.

Parikshit and the fear of death

There was a king who heard that he was going to die in a week, and so he gave up everything and sat and meditated and realized God within one week. Mother says that if we have that kind of intensity, even one moment is enough. Even though Parikshit was very detached, very intense to realize God, he was also very afraid of death. Nothing wrong with that. In a way, it's good to be afraid of death because that energy of fear will give us a lot of intensity to do spiritual practice. So what did he do? He did a very interesting thing. He heard that he was going to die by a snakebite on the seventh day hence, so he had a pillar constructed, a very tall pillar. It must have been fifty or a hundred feet tall. On the top of the pillar there was a room, and there was no way to get up and down the pillar, except by a rope. That's how he got up there. He was sitting in the room doing his meditation and whenever food was to be given to him, he used to lower down a basket and then he would pull it up with the fruits and other things. That's how he was eating for these seven days. He had stationed around the bottom of this pillar his entire army, so if any snake comes, you know what's going to happen to the snake.

Well, what happened? The snake that was destined to

bite him was no ordinary snake. He was a very smart snake. The snake turned himself into a little worm, not even an earthworm, a tiny worm. And got inside—maybe it was a mango—one of the fruits that were going to be sent up for breakfast on the seventh day, climbed in there, bored a little hole in the mango, or it must have been an apple. When Parikshit lifted up the fruit and he was about to bite into it, the worm poked out its little head, smiled at him, turned into a snake and bit him. Then he was gone, finished. You can't avoid it. When it's your time to go, you may do anything. You may be up in the sky or under the earth or in your room or on the highway or you may be anywhere, when your time's up, you have to go. Nothing wrong with that. Everybody has to go.

So we are going to read some of Bhartrihari's verses. Each one is a gem. When we are reading this, don't listen to it like some poetry or some philosophy. Try to take each one into your heart, because that's what they were written for. They are to wake us up, just for a moment at least to get a glimpse of the nature of maya because we are so deep asleep in it. It's unbelievable how deep asleep we are.

> "Old age looms ahead frightening men like a tigress. Different diseases afflict the human body like enemies. Life is flowing away like water running out of a leaky vessel. Still how wonderful that man goes on doing wicked deeds!"

This is not to say that there is nothing good in life or that we shouldn't enjoy life, but we should understand this side of life also. Spiritual life means to understand everything, not just to be enamored and ignore the true nature of things. We have to see the nice side of life, but we have to see the other side also, the painful side of life—both sides of the coin. That's real wisdom. Especially for us, most of us who are only used to looking for the pleasant side, either seeking the pleasant side or only noticing the pleasant side, this is very necessary so that we see things more balanced.

> *"Manifold and transitory in nature are the enjoyments, and of such is this world made up. So what for would you wander about here, O man? Cease exerting yourselves for them, for if you put faith in our word, on its supreme foundation, the Reality, and concentrate your mind, purified by quelling hope with its hundred meshes, free yourself from desire."*

Desire makes us run after all these transitory things. Even though we may not get what we want, hope keeps it going. What he's saying is, have faith in the words that I'm telling you now. They are born out of my experience of Reality. Give up hope in your desires so that your mind becomes calm.

> *"There is one enjoyment, and one alone, lasting, immutable, and supreme of which the taste renders tasteless the greatest possessions, such as the sovereignty of the three worlds, and established in which the gods Brahma, Indra, or the others appear like particles of grass. Do not set your heart on any ephemeral enjoyment other than that."*

So spiritual life doesn't mean giving up enjoyment. It just means that you want a promotion. You're not satisfied with the enjoyments that you are getting. Somebody's got an ordinary Chevy, next they want a Benz, then a Rolls, and after that what do you go for?

(Voice from audience) "A limousine."

—Limousine. Okay. I think next week you should sit op here on the stage. You are having all the good ideas!

So, that's nature: we have a little house, then we think it would be much better if we had a bigger house. Then we get the bigger house, and then that's not enough, "I wish I had a bigger one." Then you see someone who has even a bigger one, "Oh, that wasn't enough, I want a bigger one." How far can you go? That's just the nature of things. There is no end to enjoyment, there's no satisfaction. There can never be. So this is what he is saying: there is one enjoyment, only one enjoyment, that will satisfy you forever and that will make even the position of being the highest gods in the universe look like grass.

That's what Mother says. There's one song where Mother is describing her experience and she says,

> *"I saw everything as my own Self, and the whole universe as a tiny bubble in my own vastness."*

That's the experience. If one wakes up from this sleep, then you see the whole universe as a tiny bubble in your eternal vastness. That's the enjoyment of supreme bliss. That's the aim of spiritual life. So he is saying, "Don't run after anything else but that. Don't waste your energy. Don't waste your time. Don't get into all these complications of maya."

> *"Where in some home, there once were many, there is now one; and where there was one or many, there is none at the end."*

Understand that? In one home there were so many; then there was only one, and then after some time, even that one wasn't there anymore.

*"This is the process in which expert Father Time plays
his game on the checkerboard of this world with living
beings as the pieces to be moved, and casting the two dice
of day and night. Daily with the rising and setting of the
sun, life shortens, and time is not felt on account of af-
fairs heavily burdened with manifold activities. Neither
is fear produced at beholding birth, death, old age, and
suffering. Alas, the world has become mad by drinking
the wine of maya."*

Life is going away every day, every night. Life is getting
shorter. We are so busy with so many things, we don't even
notice it. We are drunk with the wine of maya. This is what
he is saying. Even if we don't have much suffering, we should
go—this is what Mother says—go somewhere where there is
suffering so that we can understand the nature of this wheel
of time—how merciless the law of karma is. When you see
people that are really suffering, think, "That could happen
to me also."

*"Seeing even the same night to be ever following the
same day, in vain do creatures run on their worldly
course, persevering and busy with various activities set a
going secretly by their mental resolves. Alas, through in-
fatuation, we do not feel ashamed at being thus befooled
by the cycle of birth and death with occupations in which
the same particulars repeat themselves again and again."*

A cow always goes on chewing the same cud again and
again. Our life is like that: we go on doing the same things
again and again. We go on having the same experiences again
and again, but still we go on. We don't think of trying to go
any higher than our ordinary mundane life. This is maya.

"Those from whom we were born, they are now on intimate footing with Eternity."

Means they are long dead.

"Those with whom we were brought up have also become objects of memory. Now that we have become old, we are approaching nearer to our fall day by day, our condition being comparable to that of trees on the sandy bank of a river."

If a riverbank is sandy, and there is a tree growing there, what will happen to the tree?
(*Child's soft voice*)—"Die."
—And when it dies, what will happen?
—It will mix with the sand.
—It will fall down, right?
—It will decompose, I think.
—And decompose, right. Like that, we are on the sandy bank of the river of time, because there is no firm bank on the river of time. The river of time is wearing away the sand under the roots. Finally the tree is going to fall down and decompose.

"Now a child for a while, and then a youth of erotic ways, a destitute now for a while, and then in abundance, just like an actor makes at the end of his role, when diseased in all limbs by age and wrinkled all over the body, his exit behind the scene that veils the abode of death."

Now somebody's young, then they get older, then they get still older, and then they exit the scene. The world is a stage. You can remember when you were a kid. It was all gone too soon. Then all the responsibilities of being older, and then for some of us, old age has come. Then the next step is death. Then what comes after death?

(*Child's voice*)—"Rebirth."

—Right.

> "*Being agitated, Oh mind, you now descend into the nether regions. Now you soar up into the skies. You wander all around the four quarters. Why, even by mistake, you do not once concentrate on the Supreme Reality of the nature of your own Self, bereft of all imperfections, whereby you may attain supreme bliss!*"

Our mind wanders everywhere except where it should go, which is to our own Self. It's like a river that comes out of the mountains. It goes everywhere. It never goes back to its own source, but that's where is has to go eventually. We learn so many things, we know so many things, we experience so many things, and finally we reach a point where we want to get back to the source. We're convinced that there is nothing anywhere except to rest in the Self. This is what happens when we go to sleep. However much you know, however much you experience, however much you have, finally at the end of the day, you don't want any of it. You just want to go to sleep because when you go to sleep, what happens?

(*Child*)—"You're just resting."

—Right. You forget everything, because being busy with all these things is very tiring after some time. But however much you sleep, you don't feel that you don't want to sleep anymore. You just have to get up because you have to do other things, but sleep is so happy, such a happy state. That's the glimpse of the Self. Only thing is it's dark instead of light, but that nature of bliss and rest and peace is also experienced there.

At the beginning of spiritual life, it's like that. The mind will think of everything except God, everything except the Self which is what it is doing now, but it becomes even more so when you try to meditate. Then if you persist, slowly, Mother says like pouring fresh water in a vessel of salt water, it slowly displaces the salt water. If you go on pouring enough fresh water, finally there is no salt water anymore. It's completely fresh water. If you go on pouring the thought of God or your mantra or whatever your practice is, into the distracted mind, then that one thought takes the place of the many. Finally you reach a stage where you can't think of anything except God, and the mind doesn't go anywhere else.

That takes a tremendous amount of practice, but it's not impossible. Those who attain Realization or those who are called saints or sages—that's what they did. Most of them were not born mahatmas. They weren't born with concentration. Very few were born like that. They worked hard at it. The mind is a thing that can be molded. It's a thing that you can make to concentrate. It's a thing that can become one-pointed. It's a thing that can experience Brahman or the Reality. It's a great thing. It can be used for any good thing and any bad thing, even the highest thing, which is union with God, but it has to be trained. That's what spirituality is all about—training the mind.

Mother gives the example of the coconut tree climber. Those of you who have been to Kerala know there are millions of coconut trees everywhere, forests of coconut trees. How do you get the coconuts out of the coconut tree?

(Child)—"You have to climb it."

—You have to climb it, right. There is no other way. You have to climb. So suppose you are born in a family of coconut tree climbers. That means that you are going to become a coconut tree climber when you grow up. One day, your daddy is going to say, "Listen, I think it's about time that you learn how to climb up the tree."

So you get on the tree, you try to climb up, you go up about a foot, and then you come crashing down. Then you try it again and you come slipping down. Then you try it again and you kind of get discouraged. You say, "I can never get up this thirty-foot tall tree. I can't even go one foot! Forget it. I'll become something else."

Then your father will say, "No, no, you have to become a coconut tree climber. There is no other way for us. That's been our occupation since thousands of years." So what do you do? You try again and you try again. Next time you get one foot two inches, and again you come sliding down. But the idea that you have to do it, that there is no other way, that keeps you going. You keep getting higher and higher and higher. Finally, you get right up there at the top of the tree. You are throwing down the coconuts. You can just jump up and you can jump down. Took a lot of practice, a lot of persistence. So Mother says, just like a coconut tree climber's son, all of us have to try to climb the tree of the mind and reach the top which is up here—the thousand-petalled lotus where God is sitting there shining—and then when we get adept in going up and down and up and down, everything is fine. Until then, we have to go on trying, thinking that there is no other way. It's like a journey. Where? Inside, not outside.

"In old age, the body becomes shriveled. The gait becomes unsteady. The teeth fall out. The eyesight is

lost. Deafness increases. The mouth slavers. Relatives do not value one's words. The wife doesn't care. Even the sons turn hostile. Oh, the misery of a man of worn-out age!"

We don't like to hear all this, but this is the truth. These are realities. It is not Reality; it's realities, a reality, small "r."

"As long as this body is free from disease and decrepitude, as long as senility is far off, as long as the powers of the senses are unaffected, and life is not decaying, so long wise persons should put forth mighty exertion for the sake of their supreme good, for when the house is on fire, what is the use of digging a well for water?"

Understood that? When the house is on fire, then what are you going to do?

(Child)—Call the fire department.

—What if you don't have a telephone?

—Then you run to the fire department.

—What if your living in a small village and there's no fire department? Then you go to the neighbor's house.

—And you ask them to borrow the phone.

—No! When the house is on fire, the first thing you would probably do is try to get water to put it out. So if you have a tap, a faucet, you open the faucet and you get the water. What if you don't have a tap or a faucet?

—You go to the river.

—If you don't have a river, or you don't have a tap or a faucet, then you must be having a well. If you don't have a well, then...?

—Run away!

—That's what the fire department would say! No, you start digging a well. That's what it's saying. So there is no sense digging a well when the house is on fire. Like that, there's no sense trying to do intense spiritual practice or trying to control the wandering mind when you are already falling apart. Why? Because the mind is busy with the collapse. It's worried about this thing and that thing. How can it concentrate? How can it apply itself to anything? So before that stage is reached, apply all your energy to realizing your Self.

> *"When honor has faded, wealth has become ruined, those who sue for favors have departed in disappointment, friends have dwindled away, retainers have left, and youth has gradually decayed, there remains only one thing proper for the wise: residence somewhere in a grove on the side of a valley of the Himalayas where the rocks are purified by the waters of the Ganges."*

Now Bhartrihari is trying to inspire us with sublime thoughts. He's exposed the world for what it is, now what to do? Should we become sad? Should we become miserable about it? No. We should think, "What's the alternative to this situation, this condition?" He's saying that when all these things have happened and you have understood the nature of the world, then think of living in an ashram or in a hut in the Himalayas on the banks of the Ganga and doing your spiritual practice there.

Namah Shivaya.

Satsang at M.A.Center, 1994
Tape 4 - Side B

Detachment - 3

IN THE PAST TWO WEEKS, WE'VE BEEN TALKING ABOUT how we're so asleep in maya that we don't even know that we are asleep in maya, we are so deep asleep. The purpose of such books like *Vairagya Satakam* is to wake us up, to shake us and to wake us up so that we get a glimpse of the Truth. Then from there we can start to lead a spiritual life, start to do sadhana.

Story of the marriage of Narada Maharshi

There's a very interesting story about maya, about how one forgets everything and one doesn't even *know* that one's in maya and how one thing leads to the next and to the next and to the next and it gets deeper and deeper and finally, hopefully we cry out to God and we start to wake up.

You all might have heard of Narada Maharshi. Narada is one of the celestial sages. He's not a person on the earth. He lives in the subtle planes of existence. After we leave the physical body, which we all will, then we don't cease to exist; we live in a subtler plane of existence. There are many such worlds. Those are called *lokas*. Narada lives in those subtle worlds, but he can manifest on the earth. He has manifested many times. He's considered a very great mahatma, a very great sage.

One day, he was sitting in the Himalayas. He was doing tapas. He was meditating, very deeply absorbed—not completely absorbed, but very deeply absorbed. The gods, especially Indra, the king of the gods, started to get a little worried because the gods are not enlightened beings. They did a lot of good actions—they might have gone to school, they got good grades—not just going to school and getting good grades, but they did a lot of charity, they might have done a lot of Vedic worship, so much of puja, various kinds of sadhana, but not necessarily the kind of sadhana that we are talking about, that means not for the sake of *atma sakshatkara* or Self-realization, but more to gain a worldly end. In the old days, that was how people used to achieve a very difficult thing, something which they thought would be impossible otherwise. They would resort to doing tapas, doing prayers and penance, various vows and all that. The gods reached that level of existence through their tapas. But they are not spiritually enlightened beings. They are more powerful than humans, but they are not saints, much less sages.

Indra's got a peculiar quality: even though he's the king of the gods, he's always worried that somebody is after his position. So when he saw Narada sitting there doing tapas and japa and meditation, he thought, "Narada's after my position. He wants to become the king of the gods." Actually, Narada couldn't care less because he's full of God Himself—capital "G". But Indra thought like that. He usually puts an obstacle in the way of the *tapasvis*, of people doing tapas, and it's usually the same obstacle. He sends down the damsels, the dancing girls of heaven. They are called *apsaras*. He also has various other means. I'll tell you one other means he has.

There was another occasion where there was a yogi who was doing tapas. Indra got upset, and so what he did was he sent somebody down there with a basket of *papadams*. Every-body knows what a papadam is? Some people don't know what a papadam is. Well, I think last week we had papadams here for *prasad*. They're those very tasty, crunchy, kind of... What would you call that? I don't really know what to com-pare them to because they are unique. Very crispy, tasty kind of fried food, very thin like potato chips. Everyone likes papadams. So this sage, this yogi doing tapas, he had taken a vow to conquer his tongue—his sense of taste, not talk, be-cause there was nobody to talk to—but to conquer the taste so that he would eat only dried leaves, leaves that had fallen from the tree. So Indra thought of a way to make him spoil his tapas, so he sent somebody down with this basket of papadams. They broke the papadams into pieces, and the leaves where the yogi used to go to eat were all lying on the ground. He went and mixed the papadams with the leaves.

When the yogi finished his meditation and he went over there, he went to pick up the leaves to eat a few, and they had a new taste. Leaves don't taste very good. They're kind of bitter, but these were exceptionally tasty leaves. Eating those leaves, he started getting fatter and fatter. He was get-ting sleepy when he was doing his meditation because he was getting so stout. He was always thinking about the next time when he could go and eat those delicious leaves. This way his tapas was destroyed by Indra.

Of course, this is maybe a story, but these things happen to us. When we try to go higher in spiritual life, I don't know if it's Indra or who it is or what it is, but various obstacles somehow from somewhere come one after another to divert us.

So Narada was doing tapas. Indra decided to send down some *apsaras*, some damsels. So they went down there. They were supposed to distract his mind from his deep concentration. They were dancing and singing and they had their *tablas* and *mrindangam* and harmonium and all that. But Narada didn't open his eyes. They tried their best, but nothing happened. He still didn't open his eyes, so they got discouraged. They went back and told Indra, "We failed."

After sometime, Narada opened his eyes because he wasn't in samadhi, he was just in meditation, and he thought, "I must really have attained Perfection because I wasn't affected by those apsaras." He got a little proud, and he went to Mount Kailas. He wanted to tell somebody how great he was, so he went to Lord Shiva and said, "Shivaji, did you hear? I was doing tapas and Indra sent all these damsels, and it didn't phase me at all. I wasn't upset at all. I didn't even open my eyes though I knew what was going on."

Then Shiva said, "Oh, that *is* wonderful! You are really a great mahatma! You are perfect! Listen, one thing, it's okay that you told Me, but don't tell Vishnu," (because Vishnu is the Guru and the God of Narada). "Don't tell Vishnu about all this."

Well, naturally, when somebody says, "Don't do a thing," the first thing we start to think about is to go and do that thing. Mother has told the story about the monkey, not to think about the monkey. The sick person went to the doctor and the doctor prescribed the medicine and told him, "Whenever you take this medicine, don't think about a monkey or it won't work." So then when the man went home and was taking the medicine, immediately he started thinking about the monkey. He couldn't take the medicine. So if you tell somebody not to do a thing, that's the thing they are always going to want to do.

Immediately Narada went to Vishnu, and said, "Did you hear the news? I have become perfect. I am unaffected by the divine damsels."

Vishnu said, " Oh, that's wonderful! I'm very happy to hear that, Narada. I knew that you were great—now I know that you are perfect! Come on, let's go for a walk."

They started going for a walk, and they were walking along, and Vishnu led Narada into a desert. They were walking and it was very hot. Then Vishnu said, "Narada, I'm so thirsty! Can you just bring me a glass of water from somewhere?"

Narada said, "Oh, yes, Bhagavan. Just let me look around." He left Bhagavan, he left Vishnu, and he was searching around. He found a village about a mile away and he went into this village. There was a well there and at the well there was a beautiful girl. She was pulling up the water so he went over to the girl and said, "I would like to get a glass of water for somebody."

She said, "No problem. Come to my house. I'll get the glass and give you the water." So they went to the house. The more Narada looked at the girl and talked to her, the more he started to appreciate her. Finally he decided to get married to her. Maya started. In fact, it started even before that because he was proud. He had a little pride that he had conquered all these feelings. So he was in the house. He asked the father of the girl if they could get married.

The father said, "Sure." They got married, and then Narada got involved in the business world. In the village, he started a business, had three or four kids, and about seven or eight years past like this.

One day, there was a tremendous storm and the river which was near this village became flooded. It started to spread everywhere and was rising and rising and went into Narada's house also. Everybody, the wife, the children, climbed up onto the roof, and still the water was rising and rising. Everybody was getting worried. One by one, the kids were washed away, and then the wife was washed away and Narada was so miserable. When the river started to pull him away, he screamed, "Vishnu, Narayana, save me!"—screamed at the top of his lungs. Until then, he didn't even think about Vishnu or Narayana. As soon as he cried out like that, the water subsided and the village disappeared; he was standing there right next to Vishnu.

Vishnu looked up at him and said, "Narada, where is my glass of water?" Eight years had gone by in all that complicated maya. So this is what maya is all about. We started out in God. Somehow we ended up in maya. We become very involved in maya and at some point, we cry out to God. Something happens in this dream of maya. We find some loophole or there is something wrong, we don't want to continue in this dream any longer, then we cry out to God. That's the beginning of the end of the dream. Then we go back where we came from, to God.

This is possible and it usually happens due to the association with a mahatma. Otherwise, of our own accord, that doesn't happen. The blessings of a saint or the company of a saint like Mother or maybe a saint that we can't even see, some person who has left their body, could also bless us. Maybe we read a holy book that we might have read many times, but when we read it this time, it has such a meaning; it completely changes our lives. We have become serious for spiritual life.

Story of Lord Ganesh, the merchant and the beggar

This reminds me of another story. I think it's a true story although I can't testify that it's true because I didn't see it myself, but I heard like that. There were some tourists in India. They were going to various tourist places. There was a forest on the outskirts of one of the towns where they were touring. They went into the forest. They thought there must be some nice place in there, maybe some temple or something. After going very deep into the forest, there was a sannyasi sitting there under a tree. They said, "Swamiji, we are tourists. Do you know of any nice place around here that we could see?"

Then the swamiji said, "Actually, if you keep going another few miles, you will come to a village. There's a wonderful Ganesh temple there and that Ganesh is no mere Ganesh. It's not just a stone image. That's a living being."

So they said, "Oh, Swamiji, that's a bunch of nonsense. How can you say that?"

And Swamiji said, "No, I know so. I'll tell you a story of what happened there." So Swamiji said, "In that village, there were two people very devoted to Ganesh. One was a very wealthy merchant and one was a blind beggar. The blind beggar used to sit in the front of the temple the whole day long with a little piece of cloth spread on the ground, expecting a few coins from the devotees. The wealthy merchant used to go there every morning and would go into the Ganesh temple and pray, 'O Ganesh, please give me a hundred thousand rupees today in my business—one lakh rupees.' In the evening, he would come back. Usually he was very successful, so he would again thank Ganesh.

"One day, the beggar devotee got nothing to eat. He got no money. Nothing! He had a family also. His family was starving. He went to the temple. He was in tears. He went up to Ganesh and said, 'Ganesh, how can You leave Your child like this, starving? Me and my family had nothing to eat yesterday. We got no money. Why are You so indifferent to us? Why are You so cruel?'

"Crying, he left the temple. Just at that time, the merchant was going into the temple when there was a sound inside. There were two voices that were talking, one female and one male voice. The lady was talking to the man and she said, 'Son, why are you so indifferent to your devotee? Why can't you shower some grace on him? He's been sitting here for so many years.' Then the male voice said, 'You are right, Mother. By tomorrow afternoon, I'll make him a millionaire.' Who was that? That was Ganesh's Mother, Parvati Devi.

"The poor man didn't hear that, but the merchant heard everything. He put two and two together. He figured out what was going on. He was very clever. He was also very crooked. He did his *namaskar* to Ganesh, came out of the temple and went over to the poor man and said, 'I'll give you a hundred rupees, under one condition: that whatever you get tomorrow from your begging, you give it to me.'

"Well, the beggar knew that he's not going to get anything more than a few pennies, a few paise, so he said, 'This is a great deal. Sure, you can have anything I get tomorrow. I'll take the hundred rupees.' He took the hundred rupees and went and bought food for his family. He was very happy.

"The merchant couldn't even sleep that night, he was so excited. He was going to get at least a million rupees the next day. Next day he came at eleven o'clock, sat around, hung around, he was looking. Nothing, not even a penny was put in the beggar's bowl. Then he waited till noon, nothing had happened. It was one o'clock, nothing happened; two o'clock, nothing happened. He was very frustrated. He went into the temple and started to shout, 'What kind of god are You? I lost my hundred rupees believing in You!' He was abusing Ganesh left and right.

Then suddenly he felt something catching him around the neck. He looked down. It was an elephant's trunk. It was squeezing him and pulling him against the wall. Then a voice said, 'You crooked fellow. Right now you'd better scream out to your accountant. Tell him to come here.' So he was screaming and screaming and finally the accountant somehow heard about it. He came running. The voice said, 'Now, tell him to give a million rupees to that poor beggar.'"

Are you following this story? So he gave the million rupees to the beggar. And after that, because of the touch of Ganesh, this man's mind completely changed. That day by the evening, he went home, he gave half his wealth to his family, and the other half he distributed to all the poor people that he knew. He went and sat under a tree and started doing spiritual practices. He attained peace of mind. He surrendered to God and attained peace of mind."

The tourists were hearing this story, and they said, "Swamiji, it's a very nice story, but how could we believe that such a thing could happen? That a stone Ganesh could come alive and catch somebody around the neck and do all these kinds of things, talking and all that?" Then they asked him, "Did you see that person? Can you give us any proof? Do you know anybody that saw that thing?"

Then the swamiji, with a very calm look on his face— because he always looked very calm, he had attained peace of mind—he said, "I was that merchant."

More verses of Bhartrihari

This is how somebody changed from the touch of God, you could say, but many people have changed because of the touch of Mother and have led a spiritual life from that time onwards. Once we've changed and we've decided to go for something eternal, once we've started to see the world as a very transitory thing, that nothing is lasting very long, as we read those first seventy or seventy-five verses, about how everything that we are valuing so much in this world—our body, our wealth, our family, everything—is just passing away right in front of us, and we are also going to go, and that the so-called deep affection and attachment that everybody seems to have for each other also can just evaporate at any moment, then what does such a person do next? That's where we left off in the *Vairagya Satakam* last week. After exposing the nature of maya, of worldly life, and giving us a shake, then Bhartrihari continues:

> *"When honor has faded, wealth has become ruined, those who sue for favors have departed in disappointment, friends have dwindled away, retainers have left, and youth has gradually decayed, there remains only one thing proper for the wise: residence somewhere in a grove on the side of a valley of the Himalayas where rocks are purified by the waters of the Ganga."*

So once we have reached that stage where all the delusions or illusions of the world have passed off from us, when we see that there is nothing worthwhile in the world, then what is the next thing to do? Go to the bank of the Ganga in the Himalayas to do sadhana to realize God: this is what Bhartrihari did. That's why he's saying this is what we should do.

> *"Delightful are the rays of the moon. Delightful the grassy plots on the outskirts of the forest. Delightful are the pleasure of wise men's society. Delightful are the narratives and poetical literature. Delightful the face of the*

beloved swimming in the teardrops of faned anger. Everything is charming, but nothing is so when the mind is
possessed by the evanescense of things."

So all these things are so beautiful—the beautiful green
grass on the hills, beautiful poetry, the society of good people,
the rays of the moon, the face of the beloved. But once your
mind has woken up to vairagya, once you see that everything is evanescent, it's passing away right in front of your
eyes, nothing is so delightful anymore.

"Desires have worn out in our heart. Alas, youth
has passed away from our body. Virtues have proven
barren for want of appreciative admirers. The powerful
all-destroying unrelenting Death is fast hastening in. What
is to be done? Ah, me! I see no other refuge left except
the feet of the destroyer of Cupid."

The destroyer of Cupid is? Lord Shiva. Because they say
that Lord Shiva, when His third eye opened up, then Cupid,
the god of love, kama, was burnt to ashes. The meaning is, of
course, that only if your third eye opens up, only if the vision
of the Self or God-realization dawns, can kama, or the sex
desire, be completely destroyed. This is possible only in a
state of God-realization. So he is saying to take me beyond
death, in this maya that's just going by so fast, there is no
other hope for me except the Lord.

"Sitting in peaceful posture during nights when all
sounds are stilled into silence, somewhere on the banks
of the heavenly river Ganga which shines with the white
glow of the bright diffused moonlight, and fearful of the
miseries of birth and death, crying aloud, "Shiva! Shiva!

Shiva!" Ah, when shall we attain that ecstasy that is characterized by copious tears of joy."

When will be able to sit in the moonlight by the side of the Ganga crying out to God, afraid of the miseries of birth and death? When will we get that bliss of God-realization, when the tears of ecstasy roll down our cheeks?

> "Giving away all possessions with a heart filled with compassion, remembering the course of destiny which ends so ruefully in this world, and as the only refuge for us, meditating on the feet of Shiva, Oh! we shall spend in the holy forest nights aglow with the beams of the full autumnal moon."

So, what is the rueful end of our destinies? Death.

> "When shall I pass the days like a moment, residing on the banks of the Ganga in Varanasi, clad only in a strip of cloth and with folded hands raised to my forehead, crying out, "O, Gaurinatha, lord of Gauri, Tripurahara, slayer of Tripura, Shambo, giver of all good, Trinayana, the three-eyed, have mercy on me!"

When will that day come that I can live in Kashi on the banks of the Ganga crying out?

> "Those who have only their hand to eat from..."

That means those who don't even have a begging bowl. Some sannyasis, even that, they don't have. They only go to a house and hold out their hand for alms.

"Those who have only their hand to eat from, who are contented with begged food, who repose themselves anywhere, who require no house or bed, who constantly regard the universe as a blade of grass, who, even before giving up the body, experience the uninterrupted Supreme Bliss, for which yogis, indeed, the path which is easy of access, by Shiva's grace becomes attainable."

The path that is *moksha*, or supreme liberation.

'Oh Mother Lakshmi, Goddess of wealth, serve You someone else. Do not be longing for me. Those who desire enjoyment are subject to You, but what are You to us who are free from desires?

Everybody in this world—except for the sannyasis—pray to Lakshmi. In one way or the other, either directly or not, they do whatever they can to get Lakshmi, which means wealth, prosperity, enjoyment, pleasure. But sannyasis don't have any desires like that; they want something more than worldly happiness or worldly bliss. They want the bliss of God-realization. So Lakshmi, please don't come to me. Go to those people who want you.

"The earth is his bed. The arms his pillow. The sky is his canopy. The breeze is his fan, the moon is his lamp. And rejoicing in the company of renunciation as his wife, the sage lies down happily and peacefully like a monarch of undiminished glory."

See what a beautiful image that is. To a mahatma, Mother Nature is his everything. The breeze is his fan. The moon is his lamp. Detachment, renunciation, is his wife and he lies down like a king in great glory.

"Will those happy days come to me, when on the bank of the Ganga, sitting in lotus posture on a piece of stone in the Himalayas, I shall fall into samadhi, resulting from a regular practice of meditation on Brahman, and when even antelopes, having nothing to fear, will rub their limbs against my body?"

Will those days ever come when I will sit in *samadhi* in the Himalayas and I'll be so absorbed in God that even antelopes will just mistake me for a tree and rub against me?

This is the last verse:

"O earth, my mother, o wind, my father, o fire, my friend, o water, my relative, o sky, my brother. Here is my last salutation to you with clasped hands. Having cast away maya with its wonderful power by means of an amplitude of pure knowledge resplendent with merits developed through my association with you all, I now merge into the supreme reality, Brahman."

Namah Shivaya.

Bhajan as Sadhana

"At dusk the atmosphere is full of impure vibrations. This is the time when day and night meet and this is the best time for sadhaks to meditate because good concentration can be obtained."

WHAT DOES MOTHER MEAN HERE, that the atmosphere becomes impure at the time of dusk? Because at that time the sun is setting and a lot of negative activities take place after the sun sets. Negative in the sense things that are going to disturb the peace of mind of a *sadhak*. For example, all kinds of theft and subterfuge and these kinds of things usually take place at night only, and a lot of that takes place. We may not do such things but that doesn't mean that nobody does. There are a lot of people that do theft and mischief and they do it under the cover of night.

Another thing is when night comes the desire for enjoyment, pleasure, increases. In the daytime everyone has been working and at night they want to have a good time. So these vibrations are in the atmosphere and a person who is trying to meditate, it's very difficult for him. So Mother says that at that time, the atmosphere is not pure. And as we were saying that day when we were discussing these verses, the earth is not just a lump of sand and water. It is a living being. Just like we are not just a physical body, it is the most gross aspect of our being. We have a mind. There's the life force and then the soul, that's the "I", that's the real self. It's the innermost core within the body, you could say. The body is just the physical part of the self. In the same way Mother Earth, or Bhudevi as she is called in the scriptures, her physical form is what we call the earth. And she's got the life force, and she has a mind, and then she has a soul just like us. Soul doesn't have any size or shape and so Mother Earth is neither bigger nor smaller than us. The soul is just a point, you could say.

But just as our body has its changes during the day, in the same way Mother Earth has her changes also. Just imagine we were a microbe or something inside our body. You know we are not the only ones in this body. Think about it. What happens when the body dies? It's buried, worms eat it. Where do they come from? Not from outside. They're inside.

Or suppose the body is not healthy, it falls prey to so many diseases. And the germs that are already there, they become stronger. The life force becomes weaker and then the body gets sick and dies.

So suppose you were a microbe inside somebody's body and that person just turned over. You may be thinking, "Oh no, another earthquake is coming!" Or they're snoring and you may think, "Oh no, a volcano is about to burst." Similarly, we are also very minute, very tiny, and we are on the body of Mother Earth. She has her moods, you could say, her times of day. In the morning for example, some people wake up and are very fresh; they can do their meditation or whatever it is that they do. Some people, they can't get up for the life of them, in the morning. They feel so bad. Everything is so slow and sick. Some people are night people; they are full of life at night. Some people can't stay awake after they have their supper.

So our body has its times. In the same way, Bhudevi has her times also. Apart from what little vibrations we create on this earth, these little specks with all their thoughts, Bhudevi radiates in different ways at different times.

The evening times and the morning times are considered not good times for a sadhak, for somebody who wants to control the mind. A sadhak is a person who has to be very business like, that is, they have to be economical with their time. It is just like a business man who always watches to see when the peak hours are, when all the people are going to be walking by the shop; that's the time that he is going to get everything looking very nice and displayed, so that he can avail those hours. Because before that and after that, not that he is not going to sell anything, but he is going to sell the most at that time.

In the same way, a sadhak should be looking for when the best time is to do his spiritual practices. That doesn't mean we shouldn't be doing spiritual practices at other time, but we'll get the most benefit at that time. So Mother says even though the atmosphere is impure at those time, even though the worldly vibrations are more, somehow or other, that is also the best time to try to do your practices. There's some other element in the atmosphere and anybody who's been doing sadhana for some years can feel it. At that time, just before the sun rises, just after the sun sets, the mind becomes more peaceful.

What Mother says here is,

> "If sadhana is not done, more worldly thoughts will rise up. That is why bhajan should be sung loudly at dusk. In this way the atmosphere also will be purified."

Mother says that what happens during this time is that the *kundalini shakti*, the life force in us and in Mother Nature, becomes stronger. Whatever is inside us, it starts to come out. If we are predominately spiritual, we'll become more spiritually minded at that time. Our tendencies to meditate, to think of God or pray to God, or do bhajan, will become much more. We'll intuitively feel like doing those things. Worldly people who don't have any spiritual tendencies, will feel much more active in a worldly way. Their desires for worldly activity, pleasure, enjoyment, sleep, will increase much more at the time of sunset. Mother is saying that a sadhak should use that time because there is a chance that even the vasanas, the bad vasanas, the worldly vasanas, may start to increase. He should use it in the best way possible and fight against the negative forces at that time.

Most of us don't even notice these things. We get up in the morning, we go to the bathroom, we eat our breakfast, we go to the job, we come back, we do our thing and then we go to sleep. That's the life of most people. But a sadhak is not like that. A sadhak has to be very alert about everything that's going on, both outside and within his own mind. Mother's words are intended for people who want to become alert, who want to be careful and take advantage of everything for their spiritual progress.

Mother Nature has three aspects. One is *sattva*. Sattva means calm, serene, tranquil. Think of a body of water that is very calm or when you are standing on the top of a mountain and you look over a vast expanse. How does your mind feel at that time? That's a *sattvic* feeling.

Then there is *rajas*. Rajas is activity, restlessness, ambition. So this is heat, activity. The color of that is red. The color of sattva is white. And then *tamas*. Tamas is inertia, dullness, mistakes, error, sleep, laziness, indifference, adamancy, to stick on to a thing even though it's not good or it's wrong. The color of tamas is black. It's inert.

Bhajan is a rajasic sadhana. It is a sadhana with a lot of activity in it. You are using your body, you're using your mind, you're using your feelings, you're using everything. You're not turning off everything and trying to look within at the source. You're taking everything and concentrating it into one point.

Bhajan is not a sattvic sadhana because it is so active. Mother is saying that's what kind of *sadhana* is needed to fight the negative influences of the evening time. Sometimes it's good to fight fire with fire, and this is one instance of that.

"Children since the atmosphere in Kali Yuga is full of sounds, to get concentration bhajan is better than meditation."

I was thinking of this verse when we were meditating at the beginning of satsang five minutes ago, and I was just noticing all the sounds. There was an airplane flying over, there was a little kid that was crying somewhere, there was a cow that was mooing, somebody was opening and closing a door at the other end of the house. So many sounds. The birds were chirping. This is something that is unavoidable. For a person whose mind is not strong, whose mind is not concentrated, any little sound becomes a disturbance when they try to meditate. So Mother says okay, we don't have to fight against the sounds of the Kali Yuga. Let us just drown them out with bhajan.

I remember a very funny incident in Vallickavu, this was

quite a long time ago. We were all sitting together one evening, and the neighbors, who were just about thirty or maybe fifty feet away from us, started to have an argument. Well, argument would be an understatement. It was a war. They were screaming, shouting, throwing things, you know, we just couldn't believe it. Never have I heard people fight like that; it was really an all out battle. And at that time, many people were coming to have darshan of Mother. You know what she asked us to do? We had a kind of sound system there; it was not a very high tech sound system. It was pretty bad also. But she said, "Turn it up full blast." So we put on a bhajan tape and we blasted it so loud that you couldn't even hear what was on the tape! So distorted, but at least we couldn't hear what was going on at the neighbors' house either. We couldn't hear anything but noise!

When I read this verse, I am reminded of that principle of Mothers'. That's probably why she said this thing, because she was also thinking of that. So we can get beyond the noises by making some more noise. This is one reason why we do bhajan. Probably that did not occur to any of us, that's not why we are doing bhajan here, but its one reason. If you try to meditate, your mind will be distracted by every little sound. But when we do bhajan, extraneous sound is not an element at all, as far as concentration or distraction goes. Of course, the reason we do bhajan is because our heart gets into that. Our heart opens up and we get more concentration at that time than at any other time in our lives. And so it is a very effective sadhana.

"*For meditation, quiet surroundings are necessary. For this reason, bhajan is more effective to gain concentration. With loud singing, other distracting sounds will be overcome and concentration will be achieved. Beyond concentration is meditation. Bhajan, concentration, meditation, this is the progression. Children, constant remembrance of God is meditation."*

What is this *Kali Yuga* that Mother is talking about here? At the beginning of the verse, she said, *"In the Kali Yuga, there are so many sounds."* Kali Yuga, traditionally speaking, is one division of time. It's like the Iron Age. There's the golden age, silver age, copper age and all these different ages. So the Kali Yuga is the age of materialism. That is when materialism has its sway for a very long period of time. I just thought I would read one little excerpt about the Kali Yuga, which was written many thousands of years ago before it even started, by a sage who was describing what was going to happen in the future.

When he wrote this description, things were not the way they are today, by any means. The people were very *dharmic* minded. They were leading their life according to traditional ways. Their ideal was dharma, to follow their duty, to get the vision of God, to do good things all the time. A very well regulated life. So it's a wonder how accurate this mahatma was when he wrote this.

He's talking about the progression of time and he says when the Kali Yuga starts:

"Thence forward, day after day by force of the all powerful Time, righteousness, purity of the mind and body, forgiveness, compassion, length of life, bodily strength, and keenness of memory will decline. In Kali Yuga, wealth alone will be the criterion of pedigree, and wealth alone will be the criterion of morality and merit. Again, might will be the only factor determining right. Personal liking will be the deciding factor in making a

choice of a partner in life and trickery alone will be the
motivating force in business dealings.

"Justice will have every chance of being vitiated because of one's inability to gratify those administering it.
Want of riches will be the sole test of impiety. And hy-
pocrisy will be the only touchstone of goodness. Wearing
long hair will be regarded as the only sign of beauty. Fill-
ing one's belly will be the only end of human pursuit.
Skill will consist in supporting one's family. Virtuous deeds
will be performed only with the object of gaining fame.
And when in this way, the terrestrial globe will be over-
run by wicked people, the person who would prove to be
the most powerful will become the ruler.

"Robbed of their wealth by greedy and merciless rulers behaving like robbers, people will resort to mountains
and forests and subsist on leaves and roots, honey, fruits
and flowers. Already oppressed by famine and taxation,
people will perish through drought, cold, storms, sunshine, heavy rains, snowfall and mutual conflict. In the
age of Kali, men will be tormented by hunger and thirst,
ailments and worry, and their maximum age, will only
be twenty to thirty years."

This is not of course talking about right now. It is talking about from that time onwards till the end of the Yuga; it
will only get worse and worse. In the end, people will live
only twenty or thirty years.

"When, through the evil effect of Kali, the bodies of
men get reduced in size and emaciated, the righteous
course chalked out by the Vedas gets lost. Then religion
is replaced by heresy to a large extent and rulers mostly
turn out to be thieves, when men take to various pur-

*suits like theft, wanton destruction of life and so on, cows
are reduced to the size of goats and begin to yield as much
milk. Annual plants get stunted in growth, and trees are
mostly reduced in size. Clouds will mostly end in flashes
of lightening rather than pour rain. And dwellings will
mostly look desolate for want of hospitality to strang-
ers."*

This is very interesting. Have you ever walked in a house
that seemed so desolate that you would rather not be in there
even though people are living in there? This is what the sages
are saying. The reason for that is, the bad vibrations in there,
usually the miserliness of the people that live there. They
don't offer any hospitality to the people that come to their
house. They just want to get rid of them as soon as possible
or else they may have to feed them or give them something.
Or the people are always arguing in the house, so the vibrations are negative. Even though we don't know what the
cause is, we can feel the effect. Likewise, if you go to a house
where people regularly do bhajans and meditation, and they
have satsang in the evenings, you'll feel peace in their house.

*"In this way when the Kali Yuga whose career is so
severe to the people is well nigh past, the Lord will ap-
pear for the protection of virtue."*

At the end of Kali Yuga, they say that Bhagavan Vishnu,
Lord Vishnu, will take an avatar just as He took an avatar as
Krishna and Rama. He will come again in the form of Kalki.
He will make things much better. It will become the golden
age, but that's not now. It's a very very long time from now,
about 420,000 years. And of all the yugas, of all the ages, this
is the shortest one. Our sense of time is not like God's sense

of time. God's time is just like Mother Nature's time. We may plant a seed and come out an hour later and see if it is sprouting, but that's not God's time. God will put the seed and God will sprout it accordingly. It may take months and it may take a whole year. It may take twenty years to get a tree and its fruits. So the yuga system is very big from our standard of time.

> *"If bhajan is sung without concentration, it is only a waste of energy. If sung with one-pointedness, it will be beneficial to the singer, the listener and also to nature. These songs will help awaken the listeners' minds in due course."*

So we should remember this. This is very important because bhajan is a very integral part of sadhana in Mother's presence and in Mother's life and in the life of her devotees. We should do it with one-pointedness. When we sing, we should consciously try to concentrate our mind on one point. That point may be anything. It may be between your eyes or it may be on a form, or it may be on a feeling or a light or anything that you want to concentrate on. But try to get your mind to a point, and with all your feeling, try to merge your mind into that point and conceive of that as the highest thing. If a person does bhajan like that or if you feel affected by anybody's bhajans, that's a symptom that that person is doing it with so much concentration. It has nothing to do with the quality or the tone of their voice. If a person is able to awaken other people spiritually with their singing, its because their mind is so one-pointed.

Akbar the Emperor of India and Tansen the musician

There is a nice story about this. There was a great musician called Tansen. I don't know how long ago was Tansen. Four or five hundred years ago? It was when Akbar was the Emperor of India in Delhi. So Tansen was the court musician for Akbar. You must have all heard of Akbar; he was a famous king. Akbar was not a fanatic. He was a very broad-minded king and patronized all the different arts and all the different religions. Tansen's music was fantastic. There was never a musician so great as Tansen. That's why he was one of the jewels in the court of Akbar. Akbar was thinking one day, "If Tansen is so superb, what must his guru be like? Really, I want to hear his guru sing a song."

He told Tansen, "I want to hear your guru sing once." What can Tansen say? He's an employee. He said, "Okay, come on, let's go." So they went to Brindavan. Brindavan is not very far from Delhi. This is where is guru was. Brindavan is a holy place India just as Jerusalem is a holy place in the West. Brindavan is one of the holiest places in India. This is where Krishna was born and where He lived for many years. There are thousands of ashrams in Brindavan. So they went to his guru Haridas Swami's ashram. Even now you can go to that ashram and his tomb is there, the samadhi is there and there is a tremendous presence, a tremendous peace in those environs.

They went there and Akbar had dressed up just as a commoner. The swami was sitting there in his room—they walked in and bowed down and sat there. Haridas looked at Akbar and said, "Oh, the Emperor has come." He understood who he was immediately through his divine vision. Akbar kept making signs to Tansen to ask the guru to sing a song. But you know, it's not proper to ask a mahatma to sing songs.

Tansen was very intelligent, so what did he do? He sang a song that Haridas had taught him, but he made some mistakes. So Haridas sang the same song in the correct way to show him how to sing it. And when Akbar heard that song, he went into ecstasy.

Then the two of them took leave of Haridas and went back to Delhi. All the time Akbar was thinking about the bliss that he experienced from that song. He called Tansen the next day and said "Tansen, I can't forget the bliss I got from that. I want you to sing that song again for me." Tansen sang the same song, and Akbar just sat there with a straight face. When it was finished, he said, "I don't feel anything. What's the problem? It was the same song." Then Tansen said, "Maharaj, if you don't get angry with me, I'll tell you what the problem is." Akbar said, "Okay, tell me what it is." He said, "My guru was singing to please God. I am singing to please you."

Singing to please God instead of singing to please the audience, it's quite a different thing. It may be very beautiful, it may be very nice, but there is no comparison It's like the difference between day and night.

So when we do bhajan, that should be our goal, that we should have so much concentration that we'll get absorbed in God, and everybody around us also will feel that love and that absorption in their heart.

Namah Shivaya.

Satsang at M.A. Center, 1994
Tape 5 - Side B

Food and Sadhana -

BEFORE THE TOUR WE WERE READING MOTHER'S "For My Children", the little book of three hundred verses, and we had gotten up to the hundred and sixty-sixth verse. That was the chapter on selfishness. Now we are up to the next chapter which is about food.

> "Without forsaking the taste of the tongue, the taste of the heart cannot be enjoyed."

This is a very mystical expression, as are all of Mother's expressions. Food is very important, to say the least. Life depends on food. If you look at the animal kingdom, most of their life is spent searching for food and the rest of it is sleeping. Most of us earn a living in order that we can eat, and secondarily, to enjoy and survive having a house and other amenities. But the main purpose of money is life, food. Many people spend hours cooking and cleaning up after cooking, and also going and purchasing things for cooking. Mother is not knocking food. Food is considered as a manifestation of God. Food is Brahman; this is what the *Upanishads* say. But she is saying that, even though food is important, taste is not the most important thing; it is not as important as food. This verse is more about the taste rather than the food.

Man is not just a physical body that survives by food. He's got five sheaths, he's got five bodies called *koshas* in Sanskrit. Just like an onion has rings around the center, in the same way around the *Atman*, around the "I", the being, the soul, there are five layers.

The outermost layer is the gross body, the physical body that's made of food. That's called the *annamaya kosha*, the kosha that's made of *annam*, food. Then there is the *pranamaya kosha*, the layer or sheath that's made of the life force, the force of life in us. Then *manomaya kosha*, that is the part of us that's always thinking and feeling, in other words the mind, the static, or the noise that goes on inside. And then when that same organ, the mind, is used to think about a specific thing, to discriminate, to understand, to decide, to make a decision, it's called the *vijnanamaya kosha*, the intellect. It's the same inner organ, the mind, but its function is, at that time, to understand. And when we experience some happiness due to our sense life, that happiness is coming not from the sense objects but from something called the *anandamaya kosha* or the body of bliss. When you go to sleep you are so peaceful and happy, you don't want to wake up, and that bliss is coming from the *anandamaya kosha*. When you get something that you desire and you feel so happy, that bliss is coming from the *anandamaya kosha*, the sheath of bliss.

But the innermost being, the subject of all these things, the core of all these things, is the 'I', and that's the soul, the Atman. That is more important than any of these. When the Atman leaves the body, when the soul leaves the body, all this is left behind. The physical body is left behind, and the life force, the mind, is taken with, to occupy the next body. But the essence of it is our real Self, that's the Atman, that's the "I" that shines in us. And that "I", it's always there, it is always quite perceptible to us, but it is mixed up with these five other things. When you're listening to a group of people singing, a chorus, and you know one of the people in the chorus, you can hear their voice but you can't really distinguish it, you can't separate it from the rest of the voices. So the voice of "I" is always there within all of us, at every moment, but it is mixed up with these other bodies.

Mother says that the physical body which is made of food is not the most important thing. The most important thing is who we are, the "I", the Atman. But our sense life keeps us occupied almost all of the time, so we are quite unaware of that truth, the immortal bliss of our own Self—the Atman. Our mind is always directed to the outer world. Unless there is a certain amount of withdrawal from sense life, we can't perceive the taste of our real Self, because we are completely immersed in the things outside.

You know, many people reach a stage in their spiritual evolution when they feel that way. They are just not satisfied with what's outside. Then they start to look inside, and at that stage, they might experience something through someone's association like Mother's. What do they experience, what is it that they are so intoxicated about? When people get up from Mother's lap, that look of bliss on their face...they never look like that at other times. There is something that they are experiencing at that time. They got a glimpse of something. At that time, if you'd just go over to them and say, "Hey, can you tell me what time it is?" then they may not even look at you. They don't want to be outward; they don't want to have to look outside. Even though their whole life is outside all the time, at that moment their mind is going deep within and they are tasting the peace and bliss that's got from Mother's presence. Even during a good bhajan, if somebody knocks you and says, "Shall we go outside and have a talk?" you won't even look at them. Why?

Because the mind is going beyond the physical body, beyond the life force, beyond thinking, beyond the intellect. It is touching the Self; it is getting near to the inner reality. So when you start to experience that, then you feel as if your sense life becomes a distraction.

Mother is saying that, it's also true that by reducing our sense stimuli, we can experience what is inside. If we spontaneously get it from grace or from a mahatma's presence, it reduces automatically. But it can also be the other way around, that through a certain amount of sense control, we can experience that which is inside us.

Going within, beyond the physical body

"Without forsaking the taste of the tongue, the taste of the heart cannot be enjoyed."

If we always look outside, we cannot experience the bliss which is inside. Mother says that the bliss is in the heart, meaning not the physical heart, but the core of one's being, the place where the Atman resides. There is a saying: "Where there is Rama, there is no *kama*, and where there is kama, there is no Rama." So what does it mean? Kama means desire, or you could say worldly enjoyment. So where worldly enjoyments are, and where desire is, at that moment, we cannot talk about the presence of God. They are two opposite ends of the pendulum, so to say. And when you are talking about God, at that moment, or when you are experiencing God, at that moment there can be no desire or external worldly enjoyment.

"It is not possible to definitely state that this can be eaten and this cannot be eaten. Depending on climatic

conditions, the influence of the diet on us will also be changing. The types of food avoided here may be useful in the Himalayas."

According to realized people like Mother and the ancient *rishis*, this world has a dual aspect. There is a physical world, no doubt, but all the physical objects also have a subtle vibration. You know, in the past twenty-five, thirty years, that word has become very in vogue: "vibration". It is not something new. That was sensed thousands of years ago by the ancient sages, that everything has a vibration and everything receives vibrations also. It is not just that everything is radiating, it's like a two way radio, not an ordinary receiving set. We are sending out vibrations, we are receiving. Not just human beings, everything: places, foods, people, thoughts, actions, words, they all have vibrations. The whole universe is a vast network, you could say, a vast matrix of vibrations, all based on a vibrationless substratum which is called God or Brahman.

These vibrations were basically divided into three categories, called *gunas*. Many of you might have read the *Bhagavad Gita*, and the philosophy of the gunas is nicely explained there.

I am going to read a few of the verses from the *Gita* so you get some idea of what these three *gunas*, or qualities, or vibrations are like. One is the *sattvaguna*, that's the *guna* of peace, harmony, happiness. Then there is the *rajoguna*, that's the guna of activity and also disturbance. Then the third one is the *tamoguna*, that's the guna of inertness, dullness, laziness, mistakenness.

The gunas in actions and in people

So we are starting out with actions that are of different kinds of gunas.

"An action which is ordained, which is free from attachment, which is done without love or hatred by one not desirous of the fruit, that action is sattvic."

In other words, an action where one is not attached to the results and one is balanced and calm, that kind of action is *sattvic karma*, sattvic action.

"But the action which is done by one longing for pleasure or done by the egotist, which causes much trouble, that is declared to be rajasic. The action which is undertaken from delusion, from mistakenness, without regarding the consequences, the loss, the injury and the inability, that is declared to be tamasic."

That means, when our mind is covered with dullness, that we don't take into consideration all these things, we are mistaken, and then we do an action, that's a tamasic action.

"Free from attachment, not given to egotism, endued with firmness and vigor, unaffected in success and failure such a person is said to be sattvic."

Now we are talking about people.

"Passionate, desiring to attain the fruit of action, greedy, cruel, impure, subject to joy and sorrow, such a person is said to be rajasic."

Most people in the world are rajasic. Not many people are sattvic, people who are free of attachment, they have no egotism, they are balanced in success and failure. How many of us are like that? That is what we are aiming for. The closer we get to the sattvic nature, the closer we are getting to our real Self, the Atman.

> "Unsteady, vulgar, unbending, deceptive, wicked, indolent, descending and procrastinating, such a person is tamasic."

These are the different kinds of people, and when we hear this or when we read this, we can see inside ourselves where we fall. None of us are completely sattvic or rajasic or tamasic; we are made of a mixture of these things. So what the idea of learning this is that we should weed out the lower two, the tamasic and the rajasic qualities, and become purely sattvic.

Mother says a sattvic mind is like a calm lake, that you can see the reflection of the sun, or you can see the pearl or the gem that is shining on the bottom, because it is so calm. The rajasic mind is like the broken surface due to the wind and the waves, so you can't see anything but broken images. The tamasic mind is like thick muddy water. Nothing can be seen.

The importance of the mind

When Mother is saying that different foods should be eaten and shouldn't be eaten, she's not saying what is good for your health and what is not good for your health. There are plenty of people that can tell us that, it's a big industry. But not everybody knows what is good for us spiritually, what should be eaten for our spiritual good, to make us sattvic, and what we shouldn't eat, what will make us more rajasic and tamasic. And really speaking, nobody is concerned about that at all except spiritual aspirants. Spiritual aspirants are concerned more about their mind than their body. They know that the body is perishable, it's going to go any moment. We may walk out the door and that's the last anybody will see of us. As soon as we are born, we are put in the queue, we have our ticket to go, to leave the world, but we don't know what number we have.

The body is here today and gone tomorrow. But the mind, the mind is the important thing, more important than the body, because the mind will continue in the next birth. Whatever body we may get, still the same mind will be there. And the more sattvic the mind becomes, the closer we get to perceiving the Atman. And then this business of being born and then dying and being born and dying will be over. It will be like waking up from a long bad dream. The bliss that we are always looking for in this world, we will find it in that state, we will find it in our own Self. So it is most important that we purify our mind, make our mind sattvic.

So Mother says, while we are living in this world of vibration, we should try to eat only sattvic things.

What is sattvic food is the question? It is also in the *Gita*, and here are the verses about that:

> "The food which is dear to each person is also three fold. Foods which increase life, energy, strength, health, joy and cheerfulness, which are savory and oleaginous, substantial and agreeable, are dear to the sattvic people. Foods that are bitter, sour, salty, excessively hot, pungent, dry and burning, are loved by the rajasic, causing pain, grief and disease. Food which is stale, tasteless, putrid, rotten and impure is dear to the tamasic."

(*Laughter*) Yes, there are different kinds of people and everybody's got their own taste. So these are the different kinds of foods, basically.

But what Mother is saying is, sometimes a thing that's one guna may change according to climate. For example, take tea. Tea in a hot climate like in south India is rajasic; it's a stimulant, a strong stimulant. But if you live in Tibet where it's very cold, you have to drink tea or you can't survive. Also they don't have any vegetables there, they have barley but practically no vegetables, so they eat meat. Meat is generally considered tamasic, but in Tibet where there is no other way to live, it is not tamasic at all; it is what gives you life.

Having this in mind, Mother is saying, you can't definitely say this is good and that is bad; it changes according to the climate. What's good may have to be avoided there and vice versa. But in general, these categories apply. We should try to learn what is sattvic, what is tamasic, what is rajasic and try to limit ourselves to what is sattvic. That is, if we are really serious about making spiritual progress.

All these things that Mother is talking about is for serious people. The books that have been published, the words that she said, they are for serious sadhaks, serious aspirants, not just those who are dabbling in spirituality, for whom it's just fun, or it's nice, or it's a pleasure. No. It's those who feel, "Oh, I may die any day, I haven't realized my Self, I haven't really attained happiness. What is the solution? I'm going to get old, I'm going to get sick, I'm going to die; all these things are going to happen to me too. Isn't there some way out?" You know the story of Lord Buddha? Everybody knows that story. He thought everything was fine, life is going to be a festival till the end, he is going to be young and healthy, have a good time. Then what happened? What happened?

Purna?

(Purna) —He saw old and sick people.

—Right. Anything else?

(Purna) — He saw a *sadhu.*

—He saw a *sadhu,* and he saw a dead person also. Then he asked his attendant, "Is this just for them that these things happen or is it gonna happen to me too?" Then Channa, his attendant, said, "Everybody gets sick, everybody gets old, everybody dies, even you, even your wife, Yasodhara, even the king, everybody." Then he said, "Oh, I feel sick, take me back to the palace." He started thinking, "What is the way to escape from this? I don't want to go through that, that's horrible." And he started thinking about the sadhu who was sitting under the tree. He was meditating, he was trying to escape from the inevitable. So he decided that, "This is the way for me," and he left.

I'm not saying that we all have to leave everything and go and sit under a tree and meditate until we attain enlightenment. That is not the point. Seriousness is to look at the way life is and to not get lost in maya, but to see the seriousness, the necessity of spiritual life. If that's not there, at least think what you got from Mother's presence, the satsang, what about the bliss, the joy, the peace, that unique feeling you got in Mother's presence when she was here, when spiritual life became a reality instead of just a hobby.

These words are for such serious people.

Control of hunger

"When one sits to eat food, he should proceed only after praying to God. This is why a mantra is chanted before eating. The proper time to test our patience is when food is in front of us."

This is a spiritual practice, that is what Mother is saying, to chant your mantra, to remember God before eating. In other words, to sit still even though your mouth may be watering, and think of God. It's a great tapas, it's an austerity, it's very difficult, when something is right in front of you that you want to enjoy, and you say, "No, wait a minute, I am going to think about God or I am going to meditate." That is the time to do it. One's character is tested in the face of hunger. You can really tell what a person is when they are hungry. It's said that even some saints, even saints, may throw away everything for the sake of their belly. It is such a powerful urge, the urge of hunger.

Many of you might may have read the story of Kuchela, the devotee of Krishna. When he and Krishna were young men, they were sent out into the forest to collect wood for their guru, and the guru's wife had given a packet of something to eat so that while they were out there they would have a little snack. But unfortunately, it started raining cats and dogs. They got stuck out there, they couldn't get in, they took shelter in the trees. Krishna was in one tree and Kuchela was in another tree. Kuchela started feeling very hungry. He knew Krishna was Bhagavan, he knew Krishna was Vishnu, Lord Vishnu. Even then, he started eating, he didn't even ask Krishna, "Hey, are You hungry, You want something?" He started eating and it was getting less and less, and when it was beyond the fifty-percent mark, he continued, ate the whole thing, he didn't give anything to Krishna, didn't say a word to Krishna. And, you know, for many years after that, he lived a life of poverty. Finally, of course, he got Krishna's grace and he became very wealthy, but it was only when he was an old man. So, even though he had that consciousness of God, even then, his belly got the better of him.

I know, I had an experience like that. I kind of feel shy

to talk about it but I feel that it's of some value, that's why I'm telling this. I was serving somebody, an elderly person. He had an acidity problem, acidic stomach, so he liked sweet yogurt, yogurt before it turned sour. I was not sick but I also liked yogurt before it turned sour. So this gentleman, he had gone to a temple and he was going to come back for lunch and I arranged his food. When I opened the cupboard, I found that there were two little pots of yogurt. One was very sour, one was sweet. Well, he didn't know that there were two. So, before he got there, I gobbled down the sweet one. For all my respect and all my good intentions—I was serving this person—but that taste, you know, it got the better of me. My stomach, my tongue, they got the better of me. This always used to happen at that stage of my life, that whenever I had made a big mistake, I would get clobbered on the head the next minute. He came, sat down, had his lunch and at the end he was eating the yogurt and said, "Uh, this is so sour. Wasn't there any sweet yogurt here? I can't believe there was not sweet yogurt here." So I had to admit what I did. He said, "That's very nice, you are a great sadhak, a great devotee." Of course he was not Bhagavan Sri Krishna so I didn't have to suffer too much for it, but I learned a life long lesson not to do that, to be aware of how the tongue makes us its slave and we throw away our discrimination.

On the other hand, there is the story of the golden mongoose from the *Mahabharata*—many of you know that story—where the great king Yudhisthira of the Pandavas performed a big Vedic sacrifice, and gave away millions of dollars. He gave so many gifts away to thousands of people, and it was the talk of Delhi. It was actually Old Delhi in those days, it was called Hastinapura. At the end, just at the end of this sacrifice, a mongoose came and it rolled in the dirt where this whole ceremony had been performed. Everybody saw this there, wondering, "What a strange creature this is," and when it got up, they noticed once side of the body, half the body, was a beautiful gold color, and the other half was just an ordinary brown color. So they asked the mongoose—one of them had *siddhis* and they could talk to animals—so they asked the mongoose, "You're the strangest looking mongoose. How did you get gold on half your body and your ordinary color on the other half?"

He then told this story, which I am going to tell in a very abbreviated form. Some years ago, there was a terrible famine and he had been wandering around in the country looking for something to eat. There was this poor family who were about to die from starvation. Somehow they got just a little bit of wheat, and they powdered it and made it into flour, and they made a few *chappatis*. They were just about to eat—you can imagine how hungry they were at that time. Just imagine: you haven't eaten for about two or three weeks, you're trembling, you're about to collapse, you're so hungry, raging fire is in your stomach. And then, you get three or four pieces of bread...

Just at that time, three guests arrived one after another. To each guest they gave one piece of bread then the next guest came, and so on. Finally there was nothing left. At that moment, when they gave away the last piece of bread, all of them attained a very high stage of realization, and they were liberated at that moment.

That mongoose, he went over to eat the crumbs that had fallen down from the mouth of these people. After eating the crumbs, he just lay there for a moment and when he got up, half of his body was gold. He was so enamoured of the gold, that nice color, that he wanted to get the other half also to match. So he used to go to all these great places of pilgrimage and where people were doing big pujas and doing a lot of charity and selfless service and all that, and then he would roll on the ground where they were doing these things, and then look to see if the other side had become gold. So he told Yudhisthira the king, "This big thing where you gave away all these millions of dollars, and you gave so many gifts to so many people, it's nothing compared to these people who only gave away three pieces of bread."

This shows the greatness of being able to control hunger. Only a great person can do that.

> *"An ascetic need not wander in search of food. The spider weaves its web and remains in its place. It does not go anywhere searching for food. Its prey will get entangled in its web. Likewise, the food for an ascetic will come to him through God, but he must be a man of total surrender to God."*

We are talking about a sannyasi, we're not talking about most of us. But a real sannyasi, a person who has left everything of worldly life and lives only for God-realization, such a person should not even think about their food and where it is going to come from. They need not make any effort. If they are thinking all the time or they are making effort all the time to realize God, the food has to come to them.

God looks after His devotees

Mother used to tell this story about the man who heard this teaching at a satsang and decided he was going to test it. Remember that? This man decided he's going to see whether God is really going to feed him if he doesn't make any effort. So he thought, "Not only should God bring the food to me, God should put it in my mouth also; then only I will believe." So he was sitting in the village in his hut, and he was doing his mantra and remembering God all the time. Then he thought, "This is no good, if I'm sitting here, somebody may just walk by and they'll see me and they'll think, 'Oh, poor fellow, maybe he didn't eat today? We should give him some food.' I really have to get away from the village. I'll go deep into the forest." So he went into the forest and he was sitting under a tree. He was doing his mantra.

Then he heard some kind of uproar going on at the other edge of the forest and as it got closer and closer, he could hear there were a bunch of rowdies. Thieves. They had just committed a big robbery and were coming into the forest. He thought, "They may kill me!" He climbed up into the tree. He was sitting up in the tree and was watching what was going on, and the robbers came and they put all their bags of the things they had stolen down there and then they took out their lunch.

Just then one of them said, "Let's go and take a bath in the river that's nearby and we'll come back and then we'll enjoy our lunch." So they left the place and came back after bathing. Just at that time, the man in the tree sneezed, he couldn't help himself, he sneezed. They looked up and saw him standing in the tree. They said, "Hey, you, you come down here!" They got him to come down. Then they thought, "He saw all this stuff that we stole. He must have come down when we went to the river and poisoned our food and he's going to make sure that we all die and he is going to get everything." So they decided they're going to make him eat the food." They brought him down and took the food and pushed it into his mouth.

At that moment, this man realized that what he heard in satsang was true. Of course, the story has a good ending: the police came running into the forest, they caught the thieves and they took them away. And this man lived happily ever after.

This is not for everybody, although there has been an occasional rare householder, an ordinary person, not a sannyasi, who lived like that. Many of you might have heard of Tukaram. He lived like that. He was a saint in Maharashtra, he was a married person, he had children, he had a business. But he would always repeat the name of God, all the time he was chanting the name of God and meditating, all the time, and very little time he would give to anything else. He never worried about anything. He never worried about what was going to happen either to himself or to his family. And sure enough, he was always protected, but he went through a lot of suffering, his family also went through a lot of suffering. But still they were provided for. And he became famous. Today, there is probably nobody in India who does not know who Tukaram is.

Let us be good examples for others to follow

"In the initial stages, a sadhak should exercise control with respect to food. Uncontrolled diet will produce bad tendencies. Once seeds are sown, care should be taken not to let crows peck them. After the seed has grown into a tree, any bird can sit on it or build a nest there. Now itself, diet should be controlled and sadhana should be done. At a later stage, hot, sour or even non-vegetarian food can be eaten and it won't effect you. Children, just because Mother told you that at a later stage any food can be eaten, don't eat those foods even then. You should live as a model to the world. Then others will learn by observing you. Don't use substances which are hot and sour in front of a person affected by jaundice.

*Even though we don't have the disease ourselves, we
should have self-control in order to make others good."*

There was a doctor and there was a patient. The patient
came from a long distance and the patient had diabetes. The
doctor diagnosed him and said, "You've got diabetes," but
didn't give him any treatment. There was no prescription.
He told the man, "Come back tomorrow." Then the man
said, "Sir, I have come so many miles already and to go home
now and again I have to come back tomorrow, it will be really difficult." The doctor said, "Anyhow, I can't give you
any prescription now, so you come back tomorrow." The man
left. In the meantime, the nurse was standing there and she
said, "Doctor, how cruel you are. Why didn't you tell him
the prescription and what he should and shouldn't do?" Then
the doctor said, "Don't you see this bowl of candies on my
desk? If I had said to him, "Don't eat sugar, don't eat candy,"
then he would have thought, "He's telling me not to eat candy
and sugar but *he* is eating candy and sugar."

So also Mother is saying that we may have reached a
stage where the fire of *jnana*, the fire of wisdom, the light of
knowledge may be shining in our hearts, we might have pu-
rified our minds so much that we live in the presence of God.
In that case, whatever we eat just gets burnt up, even the
subtle part of it gets destroyed. But ordinary people cannot
even conceive of that, their minds are completely influenced
by what they eat; so we should make a good example for
them. They may look up to us for so many reasons; so for
their sake, we should be making a good example even in our
food.

I'll read a little more about what the *Gita* says about being a good example.

"Whatsoever a great man does, that alone the other men do. Whatever he sets up as a standard, the world follows. I have nothing whatsoever to achieve in the three worlds, nor is there anything unattained that should be attained by Me, yet, I engage in action. For, should I not ever engage in action, men would in all matters follow My path. These worlds would be ruined if I should not perform action. I should be the cause of confusion and destroy all these creatures. As ignorant men act attached to work, so should the wise men act unattached from a wish to protect the masses. Let no wise man cause unsettlement in the minds of the ignorant who are attached to action. He should make them do all actions, himself fulfilling them with devotion."

A wise person, a person who is a God-realized soul, though they need nothing, they need do nothing, they may be like an avadhuta, they are beyond all rules and regulations. Still, for the sake of the world, to set an example, they should lead an ideal life.

Look at Mother. She needs no rules or regulations. Before any of us came, she used to live out in the sun and the rain. She cared for nothing and nobody. But when the world started to come to her, she started to become, at least in her external life, almost like a normal person. For what reason? Only in order to set an example, to guide the people whom God brought to her. So also in the matter of food, even if we have advanced so much spiritually that it doesn't matter what we eat, to set a good example, we should eat sattvic food.

Om Namah Shivaya!

Food and Sadhana - 2

WE ARE ON THE 173RD VERSE OF "FOR MY CHILDREN" and Mother is talking about food and taste, how they are related to spiritual life and how we should regulate what we eat in order to progress spiritually. Even though Mother is talking specifically about food that goes into the mouth, spiritually speaking, food has to be considered as everything that goes into us through our sense organs. What we hear, what we see, what we smell, what we taste, what we touch, all these things, as we were talking about last week, are composed of the three gunas or the three qualities of nature. There is the sattva guna, which is the guna or the quality of peace and harmony which will be helpful to calm the mind down. There is the rajoguna, the quality of agitation, activity which will make our mind restless. Then there is the quality of tamoguna which is the quality of darkness, inertness, mistakenness, forgetfulness which will make our mind dull and which makes it difficult or impossible to concentrate.

Mother is specifically talking in this chapter about food, physical food, the kind that goes into our mouth. Last week we were mentioning how the physical portion of the food, the part that we see, the gross part, is the part that goes to make our gross body, our physical body. But that is not all that we are. That is only the outermost sheath of our being.

Subtler than that, internal to that, is the mind, the intellect. First there is the life force, and then there is the mind, the intellect and then the body of bliss wherefrom happiness wells up when we experience happiness. And the subject of all these sheaths, the core of that, is the "I", that's the Atman or our real being, our real Self.

Right now most of us are completely externalized. We are identifying only with the outermost sheath of our existence, although we are conscious of all these different sheaths plus our "I". There is nobody who is unconscious of the Self. The only thing is that we mix it up with all these other things. We are unable to separate the "I" from its appendages, you could say. And that is what spiritual life is all about, trying to separate the external from the innermost essential thing, the core, which is the Atman, the Self, or the soul. So we can see we are not the body that has a soul but rather we are a soul that has a body.

Here is Mother's verse:

> *"One will say that to stop drinking tea or to quit smoking is easy, yet, one is unable to do it. How is it possible for someone to control his mind if he cannot even control these simple things? First these simple things should be curtailed. If one cannot cross small rivers, how then to cross the ocean?"*

Mother is clearly saying here that drinking tea—under the heading of tea you could say stimulants, anything that is other than nourishing to the body, that stimulates the nervous system—and smoking are not good for us if we are serious about spiritual life. Why? Because we already have enough restlessness of mind, our mind already wanders so much, and spiritual life means trying to concentrate the mind, trying to get peace of mind.

Peace of mind doesn't come from comfort or wealth or nice situations. That's only a temporary peace that's dependent on circumstance. Peace of mind is the absence of thought and that can be gained only by culturing the mind through spiritual practice. Suppose you want to build up a muscle; the muscle is not going to come by itself, you have to practice. You have to lift heavy weights, increase them more and more. In the same way, peace of mind is not the birthright of anybody, its the fruit of hard work. That is what meditation is about, that is what bhajan is about, that is what satsang is about. It needs a conscious effort. If we have decided that peace of mind is worth the effort, that it is the real purpose of life, then we have got to enquire what are all the means, what are the aids to attaining that.

For such a person who is serious about it—not for somebody for whom it is just a hobby or a part time business, but somebody who has decided that's the purpose of my life and whatever else I may do, I am going to achieve that, I'm going to try to get my mind to stop wandering and to become completely still and calm—for such a person, Mother is laying down all these rules or giving these suggestions.

Tea, coffee, anything that stimulates the nerves is not good because it contributes to restlessness of mind. We may think, "Well, what does it matter? When I sit to meditate I won't drink tea or coffee." But meditation, or sitting for meditation, is only the beginning of spiritual life. That is only beginner's stuff. We have to do that a couple of times a day to get into the habit. But there should be a constant effort at trying to restrain the wandering mind. That is real spiritual life. That is meditation. Drinking tea and coffee will stimulate our mind at other times also and make it hard to control the wandering mind. Smoking clogs the nervous system. Of course, everybody knows, even the surgeon general knows, that it's bad for health. But Mother is not concerned about that in this particular discussion. She also says certain things about what is good and bad for health. Her main concern is about our mind and our spirit, not necessarily so much about our body. Our body, it came today and it will go tomorrow, but the mind is eternal, that will go on for a much longer time, until we realize our true nature, the Atman. So the body is just a temporary thing. More important than the body is the health of the mind.

Mother says that smoking clogs the nervous system, it makes our mind tamasic. It makes it dull. It makes it difficult to concentrate, to understand, to make effort. Certain foods are like that, heavy foods are like that, oily things, stale food. We read about that the other day in the *Bhagavad Gita* where foods were classified under different headings, sattvic, tamasic, rajasic. Such foods are tamasic, and smoking is a tamasic habit.

But people who lead a spiritual life say, "Oh, I can give up tea and coffee," but they can't give up tea and coffee, or smoking. They feel, "What does it matter, after all?" If it doesn't matter, then why do it? She is saying, "If it is difficult doing that, what to say of the real work?" That means giving up a physical habit is not the real work, that is just the prep work. That's not the hard stuff; the hard stuff is giving up the internal habits. You know there is a principle in nature that the subtle is stronger than the gross, that the gross has its source in the subtle. It is much more powerful. In the same way, it is our mind which is much more powerful than our physical habits. In fact, they come into existence because of our mind. The body is just an inert thing. It is an instrument of the mind. It has no will of its own.

These inner enemies, these vast oceans are much more difficult to cross than just crossing a few small rivers like smoking and drinking. And what are those inner oceans? There are six main inner enemies for a sadhak, for a spiritual person. Actually they are enemies for everybody. Though we are talking about spiritual life, spiritual life doesn't mean going away and renouncing everything and becoming a monk. Spiritual life is human life. It's necessary for everybody in order to succeed, to be happy. Spirituality is a necessity. It's not even really a choice. Ultimately, all beings come to it.

What are these six enemies? *Kama*, that's desire; *krodha*, anger; *lobha*, greed; *moha*, attachment; *mada*, pride, and *matsarya*, jealousy. These are the six enemies that keep coming up and causing so much trouble for us and for others. These are the things that will always distract us. They will always cause conflict in our lives. So we have to remember them. We have many many qualities. The mind has infinite ramifications. The sages and people like Bhagavan Sri Krishna analyzed it down to the essence, that these are the big troublemakers. These are the hoodlums, you could say, the Mafia of the mind. If you catch them, if you put them in jail, everything will be all right.

It's worth repeating what they are, but we will leave off the Sanskrit this time. Desire, anger, greed, attachment, pride, jealousy. These are the troublemakers. And each one is like an ocean. You might think you got rid of one, then again it comes up. You think, "Oh, I never get angry," and then somebody does something and you get angry. You think you are beyond all desire and temptation and you immediately fall a prey to that. You may think you are very detached, but when somebody leaves you or somebody mistreats you, you feel so miserable. Your life depended upon that relationship or that person. You may think that you have no greed. But you look at a thing wishing that it was yours. "Oh that is a nice thing," instead of being completely satisfied with what you have.

The story of Vishwamitra Maharishi's tapas

There is a story of a sage who epitomizes these first three
qualities. It's a nice story, but we will tell it in a short form.
It's the story of Vishwamitra Maharshi.

Vishwamitra was a king. One day he went to a mahatma's
ashram, Vasishta Maharshi, a realized soul, a *brahmarishi*, a
brahmin sage who had attained God-realization. Vishwamitra
was a *kshatriya*, a member of the warrior caste.

Vasishta fed him a sumptuous meal with all his soldiers
and all his courtiers. Vishwamitra was thinking, "Where is
he getting all this delicious food and all these provisions in
this little ashram out in the boonies?" He asked Vasishta,
"Where has all this food come from? I don't even see a cook.
After all, we just came half an hour ago and you served us a
ten course meal. Your wife, she is a ninety year old lady, she
could not have done all this."

Vasishta replied, "I have a cow, a magic cow, and she
gives anything you ask. Not just milk, all products will come,
ready made. She is like a fast food machine. She will give
meals, she'll give anything you want."
Vishwamitra wanted to see this cow. He saw her and said,
"Listen, a sadhu like you, a poor sage in the forest, doesn't
need a cow like this. This would be a great thing for me. I'm
a king. I have got to feed thousands of people in the palace
every day and we need so many provisions and so many
things. This cow, it's simply an overkill for you. You can get
everything but you don't need anything. So, I want the cow."

"No, I'm sorry I can't give you the cow because I need it
for my puja," said Vasishta. "She gives me milk every day
and I use the milk and the yogurt and the ghee for my daily
worship."

Then Vishwamitra got angry. He said, "No, I'm taking the cow," and tried to take it away.

There was a big fight. Between who? Between Vishwamitra and his army on one side, and Vasishta on the other side. Poor old Vasishta, who was probably about a hundred and twenty-five years old at that time. But he's got the cow on his side. So the cow manifested soldiers instead of food and the fight was on. Vishwamitra was defeated and he went back to his country. He decided, "That is real power. That poor brahmin, he's really got power, spiritual power. What's the use of being a king? I want to become a brahmarishi like him. I'll do meditation. I'll do tapas, penance."

So he went to the forest and was doing penance. What happened? In the meantime, Indra saw Vishwamitra doing tapas and he thought, "Why is he doing tapas? He wants to get my position, he wants to become the king of heaven." So he sent down this beautiful lady, her name was Menaka. She was a celestial damsel, a nymph. She distracted Vishwamitra and he ended up sort of marrying her. She became his girl-friend, I guess you could say. For how long? Twelve years! Twelve years, he did not know how the time passed, it just went by, just like that. He had a child also, Sakuntala. After twelve years, he realized what had happened, that he had forgotten his meditation and his tapas. It took him twelve years to realize that he had stopped meditating. At that time he understood why this thing happened; Indra had done this mischief. So he got very angry and cursed Menaka.

Again, he sat down for tapas. But because he had wasted all his energy with Menaka, and on top of that, he got angry, so all the benefit that he had got from all those years of meditation before that, was gone. He felt pretty miserable. "Look what happened to me. I fell a prey to desire and anger, and greed caused all this because I wanted that cow. Never again am I going to let this thing happen."

He went to another place and sat for meditation again. Again Indra sent another lady. He got distracted by her also, but he decided that he was at least not going to get angry. He didn't curse her. One thing after another was happening like this. He couldn't get over his anger. That was the big problem for him, even in spite of so much of meditation and tapas. He was standing on one toe for fifty years. He took one breath of air once in a year for his food. He never slept day or night. He was standing out in the rain and the sun. Even then, a little problem would come and he would get angry. Little, means, they weren't such little problems. Still, he couldn't control his anger, try as he may. The worst part was that, in spite of everything, Vasishta would not accept him as a brahmarishi.

Finally he couldn't bear it any more. He decided that he was going to kill Vasishta. He became so jealous and angry. He said, "If this is the only way that I can defeat him and get in his position, it is worth killing him." His mind got so perverted. So he went to the ashram one full moon night. He snuck behind the hut and was going to finish off Vasishta.

Just then, Vasishta was giving a talk. A satsang was going on. He told the *brahmacharis* and *brahmacharinis* in the ashram, "You see the beautiful moon in the sky, how it gives light to the whole world and makes everybody so happy and peaceful and cools down the heat of the day. In the same way, that great mahatma who is doing tapas in the forest, that Vishwamitra, gives peace to the world."

When Vishwamitra heard that, all his anger was dissipated. He became like an innocent child. He repented for all the bad things that he had done and went and fell at the feet of Vasishta. He held onto Vasishta's feet. Vasishta said,

"Get up, *brahmarishi*, get up! Why are you lying down? You are a brahmarishi, not because of your tapas but because your heart has become pure and childlike."

This is, ultimately, the only way our mind will become completely pure. To get rid of these deep rooted vasanas, these oceans of vasanas, we have to do spiritual practice. But ultimately it depends on a mahatma's grace, just like Vishwamitra got Vasishta's grace. We may feel that it is impossible to do, but I know something that happened in my own experience that shows that we can conquer such habits.

There was a boy living in Bombay and he was a scientist. He used to drink about thirty cups of coffee a day. He used to chew betel leaves, a kind of stimulant; maybe twenty packages of betel leaves and nuts a day. His entire salary—he was getting a pretty good salary in those days—the whole salary, except for his rent money, he spent on coffee and betel leaves and the little food that he was eating. He was never really very hungry because of eating and drinking all those things. It would be an understatement to say that he was wired. Wired means as if a powerful electric current was going through him all the time. All that stimulation.

But at the same time he was very attached to Mother. He came to Mother. He said, "I want to leave my old life. I want to live at your feet, Mother." And she said, "Okay, but only if you can give up these two habits will I let you stay here." Well, it was a struggle for him and he succeeded for a few days. Then he went to Mother and said, "Mother, I can't control myself." She said, "There is no wonder in that. You eat some sugar candy whenever you feel the urge to drink coffee or chew betel." So he was eating lots of sugar candy. He was sick of sugar candy. He was over saturated with sugar candy. But that didn't do the trick.

One day he left the ashram and went to a teashop and

he got some coffee and a packet of betel nuts and leaves. Nobody told Mother, nobody even knew. He had done it on the sly. It must have been at night or when everybody was meditating. He was meditating on coffee. So he went out to have darshan of the teashop. And when he came back, Mother called him. And she said, "You can't fool me, I know what you did. I told you that if you can't conquer that habit, you can't stay here." He felt so bad, to the core of his being, and from that day onwards, he never touched coffee, he never chewed betel leaves again. A habit that was so deep rooted, he kicked it out right then. He had that deep conviction that, "This is not good for me and I can't get Mother's grace if I persist in this." So when that got in his heart, all the way into his heart, not just in his head, then he was able to remove that habit once and for all.

So it is possible. But Mother is saying that if you can't conquer even these habits, how are you going to conquer these big oceans of anger and negative qualities of the mind?

The power of thought

Now here is something that may sound a little strange here in this western world but, we should hear it from Mother.

"In the beginning, a sadhak, a spiritual aspirant, should not eat anything from shops."

You could say restaurants.

"While taking each and every ingredient, the shopkeeper's only thought will be how to make more profit. When making tea, he will think, "Is this much milk needed? Why can't the sugar be reduced?" In this way *he will only have thoughts to reduce the quantity to gain more profit. The vibration of these thoughts will affect the sadhak."*

Here in the western world, and more and more all over the world, social life is very important. Restaurants are never thought of as a place not to go. In fact, everybody goes out to eat. I read somewhere that McDonald's make enough hamburgers to go around the earth two and a half times if they are put next to each other. How big is the earth? Mr. Iyer, what is the circumference of the earth, you are the expert.

(Mr. Iyer) "Twenty-four thousand miles."

—Twenty-four thousand miles. So forty-eight thousand plus twelve thousand is about sixty thousand miles of hamburgers in one year. That's just one food chain. That gives you some idea of how much people go to restaurants. It's awesome.

You know in the old days there weren't restaurants. At the most, there might have been an inn for travelers. In India they had *dharamsalas, annasatras,* where people who used to go on pilgrimage could rest and have something to eat. These would be maintained free by the wealthy people—the wealthier community, probably the traders—for feeding the pilgrims. Because where are they going to get food? They're walking and couldn't carry everything with them.

It's still true that the food in your home is good for you, spiritually. It's good for your body, it's good for your mind. The food in restaurants is not good for your mind. It's cooked only with the idea of making a profit. It's somebody's business. It is not out of love that they're feeding you. You know, it's like the story that Mother tells about the father and the little daughter who checked into a hotel. The next morning they were checking out and the little girl said, "Oh Daddy, the staff were so nice here! Every little thing they were bringing and rushing about and so many people were serving us and in the restaurant also, there were people all over the place asking us, "What do you want?" They were so loving, they were so kind, I have never seen such wonderful people, so sweet they were." Then the father said, "What are you talking about? After I pay the bill, you won't even see the people. The only reason they are so sweet and so kind is to get money, that's all. That's just a façade, a show. If you don't pay the bill, you will see how sweet they are!"

A restaurant, however nice the atmosphere may be, however delicious the food may seem to taste, is not good spiritually. The subtle part of that food, which is the vibration that enters your being, creates tendencies of wanting profit instead of wanting to give, becoming more selfless, sharing—that greediness lodges in our mind.

That was the first half of the verse. Then Mother tells a little story.

> *"There was a sannyasi who was not in the habit of reading newspapers. One day, an intense desire to read the newspaper sprang up in him. Afterward he started dreaming about newspapers and about the news. Upon enquiring, it was discovered that the servant was reading the newspaper while cooking his lunch. His attention was not on the cooking but on reading the newspaper. The thought waves of the cook affected the sannyasi."*

When you're cooking food, your thoughts, your vibrations, are going into the food. It is not so with a raw thing like a banana or an uncooked thing. People like Mother, mahatmas like Mother, say that cooked food becomes sensitive to vibrations. Whoever handles it, their vibrations go into the food. In a house where there is affection, that will go into the food and that will nourish the people's minds. But in a hotel or a restaurant, there is nothing like that. So that vibration will also go into the food.

Mother says it is best, in the beginning—see, that's the beginning of the sentence—in the beginning, a sadhak should not eat anything from restaurants or shops. So you don't have to follow this rule forever. But most of us are only beginners in spiritual life. Even if we've been meditating for twenty years and we have seen every mahatma that ever came to America and we've been to India four hundred times and been to every single ashram and stood on our head for so many hours, still, we haven't got a hold of our mind yet. It still wanders and wanders and wanders like the wind. So until the mind has a real, permanent peace that is not disturbed by anything, until we feel that inner bliss without any external cause, until we reach that stage of spiritual evolution, we are affected by everything. So a serious sadhak has to be careful of these rules. However unnatural it may seem, however difficult it may seem, it's for our good, if we're serious. If we are not serious, we can do whatever we like, there's no problem.

Eat with moderation

"Don't eat food until you suffocate."

How do you say that in American English? Don't stuff yourself to death.

"Half the stomach should be for food, a quarter for water and the remaining for the movement of air."

This is, of course, an ideal. I've never met a person who could follow this. It's very hard to eat a half stomach worth of food. Still we have to tell about the highest goal, the ideal. So half for food, a quarter for water and the remaining for air. This is an Ayurvedic principal.

> *"The less food eaten, the more mental control there will be. Do not sleep or meditate immediately after eating. Otherwise proper digestion will not take place."*

Here's a health advice by Mother. One thing is, don't eat so much that you are about to burst. I saw a cow once in the Vallickavu ashram. Nobody knew how much it had eaten. And you know that cows are notorious for eating themselves to death. This cow was given more and more food. A person saw the empty bucket and thought, "Oh poor cow, it hasn't been given any food." So two or three people were feeding the cow. Finally the cow croaked. It became so full, it almost exploded and died of indigestion. Some cows, if you let them out in a green pasture, they don't know what to do and they just go on eating and eating until they die. Some people are like that. The thing is so tasty that they just go on eating long after their hunger is over. Then if you bring something to them, something they like, then suddenly they have some more room to eat. I've seen it many times. You know, *payasam*, that's a favorite of many people. You've eaten this big seven course nice Indian meal, and you are about to burst, and then somebody comes with some more rice and vegetables, or *sambar*, or *rasam* and they say, "Would you like some more rice?" "No, no, I am so full, it's up to here." Then somebody comes and says, "You haven't had any *payasam*." "Oh, all right, I'll have some payasam." It must have been coming out of their ears by that time. Everybody can find some room when it's something they like.

You shouldn't eat to the point where you can't even breathe. That's because you become very dull. You know what happens when you eat too much food? You snooze, immediately. It's good if you want to go to sleep, but it's not good if you want to meditate. Mother says you shouldn't sleep or meditate after eating a full meal. Why? Because if you sleep, your digestive process slows down, everything gets shut down, and so you don't get proper digestion and then you don't get proper nourishment and then you may get indigestion. The next day, acidity. And if you meditate, what will happen? Same thing. Because when you meditate, your life force, the thing which digests the food, also slows down. It gets channeled to the point where you're meditating. Nobody meditates on their stomach, at least I never heard of anybody meditating like that. There used to be some kind of meditation where people used to look down at their navels and meditate, but I don't think that's practiced nowadays.

Usually people either meditate on the heart or on the forehead, or they visualize something in front of them. So their *prana shakti*, their life force, is kind of channeled to one place. It's pervading the whole body but you can control it, you can send it to one place or another place to some degree. Even you can send it outside. When you talk to people, if you look at a person very intently, they feel something. That's your life force coming out a bit; it's subtle, you can't see it. Some people may be able to see it, but most of us can't. So that's needed for digesting the food after you eat. You don't want to deprive your stomach of its natural processes. So don't meditate after eating a full meal. Wait for an hour or two.

This is the last verse in that chapter:

"Once love for God develops, it's like a person suffering from fever. The person affected by fever will not find any taste in food. Even though it may be sweet, the food will taste bitter. Once we have love for God, the appetite spontaneously decreases."

This is the final word. It may be a struggle for some time to control these natural urges so that we can get a glimpse of something higher than just sense happiness or sense experience. It will be a struggle no doubt, because we've had many births of living like that. But once we get some real spiritual experience, once we taste the bliss of God, or the presence of the Atman, then it's spontaneous. Then you don't feel like going for anything outside yourself; they don't make you happy anymore. They just become a distraction, a waste of time. When you start to relish spiritual practice, you like meditating, you like bhajans, you like satsang, you like reading a spiritual book, then the physical life becomes, what to say? Almost like a downer, you could say. You know, you're really immersed in a nice spiritual state, and then you have to think about cooking and eating and going to the bathroom and this thing and that thing. It becomes a headache. Many people have got a lot of time. Some people are retired and their whole life is spent in spiritual practice and they feel so happy just to do those spiritual practices.

After mental control, bliss comes

Because contrary to popular belief, spiritual life is a life of bliss. It's not a life of suffering and misery. It may be a life of suffering and misery for a certain time only. You've heard the expression, "The dark night of the soul." That's only at a certain stage in your spiritual life, that's the first stage in your spiritual life. When you've understood some things, you feel like spiritual life is really worthwhile, you start to do some spiritual practice. But because of all those habits that you had before that, that you picked up from society, from your family and from the world, you meet with a lot of resistance. It's not so easy to meditate, it's not so easy to concentrate, it's not so easy to get rid of bad habits, it's not so easy to get good habits. All these deep rooted things are there. So then you start to suffer, "Oh, what a headache this is, what a struggle this is." People see you looking very sad, going around with a long face. They say, "I thought you were a spiritual person, you're suppose to be radiant with divine bliss." Well, that's not at the beginning. Nobody gets their college degree without going through the whole school system from kindergarten up to the university. That's like seeing a child in kindergarten and saying, "Where's your Ph.D.?" "How can I have a Ph.D.? I haven't even gone to school yet."

So how can you get divine bliss unless you work for it? One of the stages is this kind of miserable condition, where you're struggling with all the grossest stuff of your personality, your past personality, your previous births' personalities. But once you get beyond that, the scum on the surface of the pond clears for a moment and then you see the clear water. Once you start to get a glimpse of your real nature, the Atman, or you start to feel the presence of God, you feel some devotion, then spiritual life becomes bliss. Then all these rules and regulations and do's and don'ts, they become very easy. When you become really deep in that, you become established in the Self or in God's presence, then it becomes natural. You just have to cultivate it. As Mother says,

"First comes the rehearsal, then the real play starts."

Sadhana is like a rehearsal and the state of bliss is like the play.

I'd like to read just a few things which are describing somebody's experience who attained bliss, because it's very rare that we find descriptions of that. There's a lot of people in the present day and age that write about their experiences. This is somebody, a couple thousand years ago, who in a traditional way went to a guru, took refuge in the guru, had the guru train him, and then experienced divine bliss. This is his description.

> *"Having understood the supreme truth on the authority of the scriptures, the instruction by the guru and by his own reasoning, with his senses stilled and the mind controlled, the disciple became motionless in a lonely place. Establishing his mind for a while in Brahman, the Supreme Reality, he got up and spoke as follows out of the abundance of his joy."*

So he steadied his mind, went to a quiet place, all alone, made his mind completely still and thought about the teachings that he had studied, and everything that his guru had told him. His mind became one-pointed and it experienced supreme bliss. Then he said,

> *"The magnificence of the ocean of the Supreme Brahman filled with the nectar of realization of the Self, cannot be adequately expressed in words, nor thought of by the mind. My mind, which has attained the state, such a state, and merged in that ocean, is now content by the enjoyment of bliss. Where has this universe gone? By whom has it been removed? It was seen by me before, but it is not. What a wonder! There's only the ocean of bliss. What is to be discarded, what is to be accepted? What's different? What's distinct in this great ocean filled*

with the nectar of infinite bliss. I do not see anything. I hear nothing. I do not know anything. I simply abide in the form of my own Atman and continue in the enjoyment of Bliss.

"My obeisance to you, O guru, again and again. O you great one, free from all attachment, the best among the knowers of Brahman, who are the embodiment of the eternal essence of bliss, the infinite, the everlasting supreme reservoir of mercy. By the bestowal of whose gracious glance, like the compact rays of the cool moon, all my afflictions of samsara have been removed, and I have acquired in a moment the undecaying state of the Self, which is of the nature of Infinite Bliss. I'm blessed. I attained my purpose. I've been liberated from the clutches of the ocean of birth and death. I am of the nature of permanent bliss. I'm full, by your grace.

"I am Brahman, which is without anything to equal it, the beginningless truth beyond all imaginations and of the nature of uniform eternal bliss, the Supreme Truth. By the play of the winds of maya, the various waves of the universe arise and are merged in me, the infinite ocean of bliss. Like the sky, I am beyond all imagined divisions. Like the sun, I'm different from the illumined. Like the immovable mountain, I'm permanent and unmoving. Like the ocean, I'm without a shore. In my great dream in the forest of birth, old age and death, rocked by maya, I had got exhausted by various afflictions which afflict me every moment. I have been tormented by the tiger of ego. By your infinite grace, my guru, you have awakened me from sleep and saved me."

Om Namah Shivaya

Satsang at M. A. Center, 1994
Tape 6 - Side B